F I R S T   E D I T I O N

Sporting Clays Consistency:
You Gotta Be Out of Your Mind!

A Shooter's Guide *to the* Mental Aspects *of* Sporting Clays *&* Life

by
Gil *&* Vicki Ash
with
Ty Adams

OSP PRESS
Houston, Texas

OSP Shooting School
www.ospschool.com
800-838-7533

Copyright © 2006 by Gil & Vicki Ash

Optimum Shotgun Performance Shooting School

OSP is a registered trademark of Gil & Vicki Ash

All rights reserved under the International and Pan-American Copyright Conventions. No part of this book may be reproduced or transmitted in any form or by any means, electronic or mechanical, including photocopying, recording, or by any information storage and retrieval system, without express written permission from the publisher.

Any mention of trademarked names or products in this text are used purely for conversational or instructional purposes only and are not intended as copyright infringement.

Published in the United States by Gil & Vicki Ash /

OSP Shooting School, Houston, Texas USA

Publisher's Cataloging-in-Publication

Ash, Gil.
  Sporting clays consistency: you gotta be out of your mind!: a shooter's guide to the mental aspects of sporting clays & life / by Gil & Vicki Ash with Ty Adams. -- 1st ed.
  p.cm.
  ISBN 0-9760204-1-6

  1. Sporting Clays. 2. Trapshooting. 3. Shooting.
  I. Ash, Vicki. II. Adams, Ty. III. Title.

GV1181.A84 2006   799.3'133

First Edition

Dedication:

To our ever-growing list of students and friends who have trusted us with their games: Your faith in us gives us the courage to go on and explore the physiological and psychological aspects of performance, not only in sporting clays, but in life itself.

Our journey in sporting clays began as competitors where we traveled and competed all over the country. We made new friends, saw new places, had loads of fun, and learned so much about ourselves and this game called sporting clays. Because of our success at tournaments, we were constantly asked how we did what we did. To those of you who had the courage to ask, we owe you a great deal. You are the ones who made us stop and ask ourselves how we did it, which led us to our next journey.

To Steve "Skippi" Brown who believed in us so much that he relentlessly searched for (and found!) physiological documentation to prove that what we teach actually works. Many times, with his belief in us and our system, Steve alone has given us the courage to go on despite the ridicule of others. This has not come without a price. Steve, for your courage to endure ridicule that came because of your belief in us, we will be forever grateful. You are an inspiration. You have given us the courage to look beyond the obvious and seek out the real reasons why things happen. It seems as though whatever path you take or whatever path we take, we all end up back on the same road. Shotgunning is a vision game and the more we understand vision, how it works, and how to apply that knowledge, the easier the game becomes. Thank you for sharing your genius with us.

After a clinic in Houston, our student Russell Ueckert shared with us his definition of genius, and we think it applies here:

Genius makes observations that others can't see.
Genius makes associations that others don't recognize.
Genius sees simple patterns when others see complexity.
Genius explains things in a way to make them obvious when they previously seemed subtle or elusive.
Genius recognizes quickly when it is wrong, and moves in another direction.

Thanks Skippi.

Contents

Introduction:	*Consistency*	1
Chapter 1	*Feel*	4
Chapter 2	*The Log*	10
Chapter 3	*Goals and Expectations*	17
Chapter 4	*The Feel Blocker*	26
Chapter 5	*Voice Management*	31
Chapter 6	*The Pre-Shot Routine*	43
Chapter 7	*Before You Can Feel*	52
Chapter 8	*Visualization*	65
Chapter 9	*The Next Step*	76
Chapter 10	*Self-Coaching and Thought Management*	89
Chapter 11	*Score Plateaus and Slumps*	103
Chapter 12	*High Intensity Practice, with a Purpose*	117
Chapter 13	*Tournament Shooting*	136
Chapter 14	*After the Fat Lady Sings*	151
Chapter 15	*Common Challenges*	155
Chapter 16	*Coaching Feel*	168
Chapter 17	*Reviewing Your Year*	175
Chapter 18	*Parting Thoughts*	180

INTRODUCTION

Consistency—10 miles. Wouldn't that roadsign be nice to see on the way to your next sporting clays tournament? Don't you sometimes wish that mastering your sport was as simple and straightforward as jumping in your car and driving from one town to the next?

In reality, most sporting clays shooters live in Erratic-ville, just like the majority of amateur athletes in any sport. Sure, they've visited Consistency. They've been for a day or two, maybe longer, but they never get to stay. It's a great place, and they would pack up the U-haul and move if they could, but every time they go, they have no idea how they got there. And while plenty of folks are shouting directions to help them, some who even live in Consistency themselves, there's a problem. It turns out that directions to Consistency are personal. While two lefts and a right might work for one person, those same directions might lead another person to Craptown. It's quite a predicament.

And this predicament is the reason we do what we do. It's the driving force behind this book. During the course of our 30 years combined experience as coaches, we made an astonishing discovery. Not only is it necessary to physically build your own road to Consistency, but arriving there is as much dependent on a mindset as any road you'll ever build. You might have started a road based on solid fundamentals, but if you never train your mind to adapt to the Consistency wavelength, you won't see it! Instead, your road will look like a dead end.

For shotgunners, there is a lot of "how-to" material out there about building a road with fundamentals. We've written a great deal about it ourselves. But there is not a lot of shotgun-specific information about how to train your brain to foster a consistency mindset. That's exactly what we intend to do here.

And while this book is primarily oriented toward shooters with sound fundamentals, which we illustrated in our book *If It Ain't Broke, Fix It!*, we also think it'll be an enjoyable read for shooters at all levels. We're sure most everyone will be able to understand the principles and strategies discussed, but actual application is a different matter. Beginners will definitely benefit more by applying the information in this book after they have a decent move and mount—after they've done the flashlight exercise so many times it's as natural as breathing.

Our main objective with this little discourse is to provide intermediate and advanced shooters with the means to create their own avenue to greater and greater consistency. For those unfamiliar with our methods, reading *If It Ain't Broke, Fix It!*

> **Flashlight You Say?**
> *The flashlight exercise is one of the best ways we've found to build a sound fundamental move with a shotgun. We've taught it in our classes, written about it in* If It Ain't Broke, Fix It! *and demonstrated it in our video* How to Practice *and* Understanding the Move. *If you are a beginning shotgunner, we highly recommend you integrate it into your daily practice. There is no better way to build a basic move and mount.*

would be helpful. For those who already have, we're going to start by telling you that you'll have to forget everything we told you in that book … at least for a few seconds at a time. See, isn't this going to be fun?

There is a secret in that apparent contradiction, and it is the golden thread that weaves all of these teachings together. We have found it to be the key to high-level performance in our sport and just about any other endeavor you can name. It separates inspired performance from average performance in many fields. It practically oozes out of all great athletes. Good musicians have it. And like most of the true keys to life, its beauty is its simplicity, and its simplicity is the reason it's overlooked by a lot of people.

We can sum it up in one word.

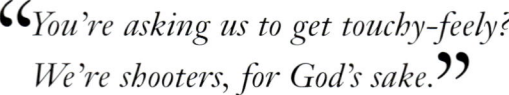

"You're asking us to get touchy-feely? We're shooters, for God's sake."

CHAPTER ONE

FEEL

Feel.

The road to mastery is paved with feel. Even so, feel hasn't traditionally been a big topic for many shotgun instructors. When we first started talking about it, we called it shooting instinctively, and a lot of other instructors thought we were peddling snake oil. Now, it seems that our sport is finally joining with many others on the "feel" bandwagon, and "shooting instinctively" is becoming more mainstream.

Shooting instinctively is the same as what we sometimes call "subconscious shooting," which is the same as shooting with feel. It is feel that allows any performer to be "in the zone." The concept is not a new one in sport, although we do seem to be breaking new ground in the way we are applying it to shotgun sports. The vast majority of modern "feel-based" instruction and mental performance books we have seen are about golf. We've studied tons of them, but there are three in particular that have had a profound impact on the way we teach. They are: *The Inner Game of Golf* by Tim Gallwey; *Golf is Not a Game of Perfect* by

Bob Rotella; and *Extraordinary Golf: The Art of the Possible* by Fred Shoemaker.

And while these are fantastic books, sporting clays is not golf. The exercises and strategies designed to increase feel in golf don't translate to sporting clays. Golf has a great number of variables in it, but we believe sporting clays has even more. Golf courses mostly stay the same once they are built; sporting clays presentations are constantly changing. With golf you have 18 different targets that are stationary; with sporting clays you can have as many as 200 that are zipping around at all different angles. It's a game with a lot of built-in failure, which encourages fear and mechanical thinking.

So for many years, we have been consumed with the process of testing the mental game concepts emerging in sports like golf, expanding them and applying them to shotgunning. We looked around and realized that virtually no one was using mental performance ideas to create a system that would work for a game with as many variables as sporting clays. So, with the help of our students and some fellow coaches, we did. This book is the most recent evolution of that system, and although it will continue to evolve, we've found that it keeps bringing us back to a higher and higher application of the same concepts, the biggest being feel.

Now, we understand the prevailing attitude in our sport. We know a good many shotgunners will react to what we're saying with something like this: You're asking us to get touchy-feely? We're shooters, for God's sake. We've got shotguns. We snort and spit and cuss and scratch. We smell like gunpowder. What kind of fruit-basket gets all mushy with a shotgun in his hands? Sure, golfers might be doing it, but have you seen the kind of clothes they get away with wearing? The poofy pants and berets? What's next, lace-trimmed shooting vests?

Well, understand that we're asking you to get shooty-feely, not touchy-feely. Touchy is up to you—it would certainly take guts to be the guy on the squad always calling for a group hug—but if you're seeking to elevate your game, feel is a must. What you've got to do is get out of your mind. That's really what shooty-feely is all about. You can still scratch, snort and spit as much as you want.

So how exactly do you get out of your mind? What exactly is shooty-feely if it's not standing in a circle holding hands and talking about your inner child? We can show you the base form of feel right now. Seriously. Pick up a shotgun (even if it's imaginary). Go ahead, humor us. Okay, now pretend to shoot a target in the air.

Whether you realized it or not, you just felt something.

Told you it was simple.

You felt tight or loose, jerky or smooth, comfortable or clumsy. Maybe certain parts of your body felt stiff or heavy. This probably registered differently for each of you, depending on your level of focus and awareness. For many of you who have trained with us, we bet you felt immediately connected to that imaginary target and had a heightened awareness that your hands were moving in concert. Or maybe you didn't feel connected but were aware of some mechanical or mental glitch that prevented it.

If you were brave enough to even allow yourself to shoot a pretend target, it's safe to say that quite a few of you had almost megaphone-like thoughts that eclipsed your feel. Does this one sound familiar? *God, I look like a jackass. I paid money for this?* Or maybe it was: *I hope no one is watching.* How about: *Maybe I should flip ahead to find the real exercises.* Anybody resemble those remarks?

That's the thing about feel. When you're deep inside your

own head, you don't have feel—you've got to be out of your mind.

Here's a non-shooting example of feel most of us have experienced. Have you ever sat down for a meal in front of the TV and got so distracted by what you were watching that by the time you finished your food, you couldn't really remember what it tasted like?

Now contrast that with the experience of cooking up a meal over a campfire in the backcountry or on an old stove at a remote hunting cabin where there's no entertainment except for some crackling embers and the wind blowing through the trees. If you're like us, you might have commented that even the simplest food somehow tastes better in places like these. But maybe it's not so much that the food tastes better, but that you're feeling it more. It's more about a change in you than a change in the food. Maybe in the isolation of the wilderness, you're actually more in tune with physical sensation. You're "eaty-feely."

And that's probably not so different from shooty-feely. When you're in a sporting clays stand, your goal should be to have the "isolated in the wilderness" mind instead of the "distracted by the TV" mind. One mind deadens sensations, the other amplifies them.

You might also say that when you are doing something with feel, you are fully in the present. It is a direct experience. Your thoughts are not in the future or in the past.

So if you are the most shooty-feely person in the world, then your mind is on nothing else when you are shooting a clay target. In fact, you have the ability to get completely outside of your conscious mind and into the realm of feel. You feel a connection to the target on a visceral level. It feels like a part of you, and every muscle in your body flows with it toward the breakpoint. All of your movement is 100 percent pure reaction to that target. You have the amazing sensation of knowing that it's dead before you pull the trigger. Here's the trick, though: you're not consciously thinking about how it feels—you're simply feeling it. You're out of your mind.

Someone who is light years away from shooty-feely probably has an inkling that he is in a sporting clays stand holding a shotgun, but not much else. He is not aware that he's leaning way back and rainbowing the muzzles over the target's line, or squeezing the gun like it's electrically charged, or moving fast enough to lead an F-16. His mind is focused on so many other things that any feel is completely drowned out. It's like he's distracted by the drama of the little TV show he's created with his thoughts.

We have found that the majority of shooters are somewhere between those two extremes of feel. That's probably why you're reading this book and that's definitely why we're writing it.

So here's the good news: feel is not some elusive quality that you're either born with or you're not. It's more than an abstract concept. We don't have the market cornered on it, and we're not suggesting that you have to come see us so we can tell you whether or not you have this mysterious "feel." You will know when you experience greater feel. When your move and mount is in complete concert with the target to the degree where you know that the target is dead **before** you finish the mount and pull the trigger, you have felt the target. This is what we mean when we say *feel*. It is trainable and can be enhanced in measurable ways. There are things you can do to create a more receptive environment for feel in your performance. We have experienced this ourselves and seen it happen in a countless number of students. The system of mental and physical training we are going to outline in this book is simply the best way we have found to put shotgunners in touch with their highest potential for feel. The really magical thing is that it also seems to have the same effect on many other aspects of life.

We guarantee that you already have feel, even though you may not be aware of it. You've been "out of your mind" at some point or another. If the exercise of shooting an imaginary target with a shotgun produced some feeling in you, turn the page, because you have what it takes to achieve consistency in this game. If you felt nothing, you're either dead, you have no nerve endings, or you've not yet been acquainted with "the voice."

If it produced an erection, please consult your local treatment center immediately.

Chapter Recap:

- Shooting with feel, or shooting out of your mind, is the key to consistency.

- Feel is exceptionally simple. Pretend to shoot a target with a shotgun and note what physical sensations you experienced. That's called feel.

- Feel is not an abstract quality that only some people have. You already have feel, and it can be enhanced in measurable ways.

- We're going to show you these ways, just keep your pants on.

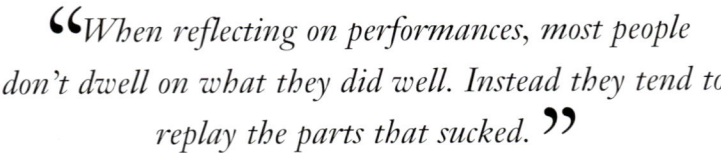

"When reflecting on performances, most people don't dwell on what they did well. Instead they tend to replay the parts that sucked."

Chapter Two

The Log

After all that about feel, how can we have the gall to make the shooting log—something so mundane and conscious-thought oriented—the subject of chapter two?

Feel is initially accessed through awareness. That's how we start coaching feel, by simply asking our students to be aware of certain elements in their game. And there is no better way to increase awareness of your shooting than by writing it down. At its core, that's all the log is. It's a record of your environment, your physical condition, and your mental state during each performance and how you felt afterward.

We've been advising our students to keep a shooting log for years. We do have a log template for students, detailing the major information that we recommend you put into the log. It's included on page 14, so have a look, but keep in mind that you can add as much information as you want.

Painting Your Patterns
The purpose of the log is to help you paint the most realistic

picture of your game. It helps you find the true strengths and weaknesses. It allows you to see patterns that you wouldn't see otherwise. That's a big thing. As you go through your year, review your log for patterns that have developed. When we look at a shooter's log, we find recurrent problems or recurrent successes and ask: why? Why do you always perform better when you're shooting in the morning? You focus great at local shoots, so why did you belly flop the first few times you traveled? Does Mexican food really help you hit fast crossers?

We think you'll be amazed that your strengths and weakenesses are so obvious in the log, and maybe a little surprised that they aren't exactly what you thought before you kept a log. It'll probably also impress you that you're such a creature of habit. The amount of sleep you get, what you eat, the time of day, how much you shot the week before—these things will play out very consistently with regard to your inspired and uninspired performances. Think of it as trying to find the right recipe for creating your "zone" experiences, or shooting with great focus and feel.

Another benefit people get from keeping a log, it helps to keep emotions in check. When reflecting on performances, most people don't dwell on what they did well. Instead they tend to replay the parts that sucked. Dwelling on suckage, as the kids might say, is extremely damaging for a lot of reasons. We'll get into it more as we talk about mental performance, but keeping a log is the first place to counter that negative instinct. Simply write down what you did well and what you need to work on. Each time you have a good practice session, each time you have a good performance, write down several things that you feel contributed to that, because in writing it down, it becomes more a part of you.

The more you do that, the more you have a true reflection of what's really there. Without a log, without a true commitment to look at your game for what it really is, you only remember the poor performances.

Getting It Write

We recommend that you write in your log after every time you play with that shotgun. That could be a 200-bird tournament or a 50-bird practice. When you're through with the practice session or competition, put your gun in the case, get in your rig, and write down how it felt while it's still fresh. *I focused well today, or I really committed to the breakpoint, or I felt good with six hours sleep.*

It's also important to include what the goal was after the last session. For example: *Last entry says I need to work on dropping teal from about 30 yards because that shot gave me trouble several times. Today, I shot 50 dropping teal at that range and began to feel connected about halfway through. I realized that I wasn't seeing the target clearly because the muzzles were blocking the flight line, and I wasn't playing far enough below the teal as it dropped because I was afraid it would get by me. Once I calmed down, moved the muzzles out of the sight line and let the bird come to the gun, the connection really happened and the targets started breaking.*

When you write down what your goals were for each session, you're giving yourself a more focused purpose for every session that follows. The log is key to helping you maintain specific goals for each practice, and that will pay off big time.

No Log, No Sympathy

In a way, this log thing is a lot like visualization, which we talked about in *If It Ain't Broke, Fix It!*. The log and visualization are some of the greatest tools we've found for enhancing performance. We pound away on their importance all the time and have for many years.

Yes, they're silly. Focused daydreaming and keeping a diary—they can't possibly help your game as much as going out and shooting a flat of ammo, right? Well, try 'em. Make up your own mind, but at least give them a chance. They aren't expensive, they don't take a lot of time, and they're not complicated.

For some reason, though, a lot of shooters don't commit to maintaining a detailed log right off the bat. Same thing for visualization. It takes a while for them to come around. Maybe they just feel kind of goofy doing it. Maybe they're too caught up in the thrill of burning gunpowder to pay notice to non-shooting training. And that's okay. After all, shooting sporting clays is fun.

"Visualization is a powerful tool because it is a subconscious picture of a desired outcome."

—*Vicki Ash*

Eventually, when they hit a ceiling in their shooting, they come to us looking for a little advice and probably a little sympathy. One of the first things we ask them is, "Are you keeping a good log like we suggested?" If the answer is yes, guess where we'll go to find a solution, to dig up the advice they're looking for? If the answer is no, sympathy is out of the question. And the main advice? Start keeping a good log.

Student after student, those who commit real effort to a shooting log, and do so faithfully, see their games improve dramatically. They gain awareness, which creates fertile ground for feel; direction, which elevates the quality of their practice sessions; and perspective, which makes them a hell of a lot more pleasant to be around.

SHOOTING LOG TEMPLATE

DATE: _____ LOCATION: _____

PRACTICE OR COMPETITION TYPE: _____

TIME OF DAY: _____ WEATHER: _____

SHOTS FIRED: _____ SCORE: _____

Evaluation (*Please Refer to Shooting Log Key*)

Score (*1-10*)

_____ 1. Sleep, *Number of Hours*: _____

_____ 2. Meals   List: _____

_____ 3. Goals   List: _____

_____ 4. General Thoughts   List: _____

_____ 5. Strong Points   List: _____

_____ 6. Improvement   List: _____

_____ 7. Distractions   List: _____

_____ 8. Equipment Change   List: _____

Shooting Log Key

1) Rate how you slept on a scale of 1–10. Waking up refreshed after deep, restful sleep gets a 10, and waking up tired after tossing and turning all night gets a one. How many hours of sleep did you get?

2) List the meals you had before shooting, including the evening before. What did you eat? How much did you eat? What time did you eat? Was the timing and content of your meals close to your normal schedule? Were they nutritious meals or junk food? Give your meals a 1–10 score. A 10 score goes to highly nutritious meals that didn't vary in portion size or time of day from your every-day routine. A one score goes to junk food eaten at erratic times.

3) List your goals for the session. If you are training, what specific moves are you going to train? How many targets will you shoot on each move? If it will be a practice session, what are you going to practice? (i.e. pre-shot routine, post-shot routine, correction routine, five pairs in a row from each station or shooting 100 targets for score.) If it is a tournament, what are you going to focus on today, based on your last tournament and your practice since then? After the session, give yourself a 1-10 score on how well you executed your goals.

4) List your general thoughts after shooting. How did you feel as you shot today? How was your focus? Did you have fun? What did you learn about how you practice, train or shoot tournaments? Based on how much you learned today and how important it is to your future shooting, give yourself a 1–10 score.

5) Address the things you did well, such as making a good plan, sticking with a consistent, subconscious routine, keeping your eyes still in the focal point or committing to the breakpoint, etc. Score 1-10 based on whether or not you're satisfied with your overall proficiency of the things you listed.

6) Address the things you intend to improve. List the specific parts of your game where you will work to increase proficiency. Refer to log entry number five and list what you will dominate in your next sessions.

7) Address the things going on your life other than shooting. List anything that caused a distraction in your focus while shooting. Score 1-10, with one being extremely distracted and 10 being free from any distractions.

8) Additional comments about equipment. Anything that has changed about your equipment should be listed here. Based on how helpful it was, rate it on a 1–10 scale.

> **Kruger's Log**
>
> *Jeff Kruger, a shooter, student, and friend of ours from Wyoming talked about his shooting log on our "Coaching Hour" call-in show. (www.ospschool.com/coaching_hour.html) He brought up another benefit we hadn't thought of, in addition to how it provided direction for his practice. "My log has helped me a lot in realizing how difficult this game is," Jeff said, "and in realizing how many exterior things going on in your life can affect how well you perform." That's why he decided to add another entry to the log template.*
>
> *"I would add just a synopsis of what's going on away from my shooting. In my personal life, and business—just a little blurb," he said. "And rate that, too, because you'd mentioned before that we've got to realize, gosh, we're human. If we've got a thousand things going on in our personal lives that are really pulling on us, it's going to have an effect on how we perform."*

Chapter Recap

- Learning (or re-learning) to feel starts with awareness.

- A shooting log is about building that awareness by recording each shooting performance, noting how you felt during and afterward.

- Among other things, a log helps you identify patterns, create a recipe for "zone experiences," and keep emotions in check.

- Write in your log after every time you play with your shotgun, including what your goals were for the session.

- Many shooters neglect the log because it seems too simple. This is dumb.

- Did we mention this log thing really helps with perspective?

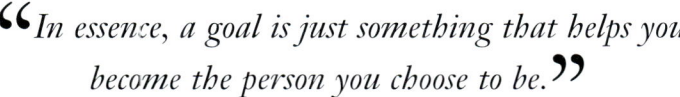

"In essence, a goal is just something that helps you become the person you choose to be."

CHAPTER THREE

GOALS *and* EXPECTATIONS

Consistency in any endeavor rarely happens by accident, and mastery never does. We're pretty sure Beethoven didn't come up with his concertos by throwing his cat on the piano, and Einstein didn't come up with $E=mc^2$ on a cold night in Germany while trying to pee his name in the snow.

The most awe-inspiring human endeavors are the results of goals and commitment. Throughout history, the people we all admire most have lived their lives on purpose, with purpose, and for a purpose. Their achievements were born out of commitment. And you've got to believe that the same goes for our little game. We definitely do. That's why goals are such a big part of our instruction.

Our first suggestion is to write down your goals. Yeah, yeah—it's more writing. We know, you picked this sport to make noise and break things, not to write essays, and we don't expect an essay. Just jot down what you'd like to accomplish. Maybe it's winning a local tournament, punching into B Class, A Class, or Master Class, or breaking 100-straight in skeet, or making the All-American team. Could be that you're a beginner and just want to break somewhere around 60 percent of the targets you shoot. Maybe, like some of the students we see, you want to be world champion. If that's true, write it down. It can be as small a goal or as big a dream as you want; we're not going to discourage it.

But we are going to ask you to do something challenging. Next to your goal, write down the things you're going to give up in order to achieve it.

Wha—? A sacrifice?

That's almost a dirty word these days, isn't it? It's got to happen though. Nobody picks up this game with an empty dance card. We know you have too much to do already, and sporting clays is not an easy game to master. That's why we believe in really defining ***why*** you're doing this. If you have the desire to compete with the best, you will have to commit a huge amount of time and energy to that pursuit. If hitting six out of ten on average is more your speed, you'll still need some practice time as a beginner. You might have to forego watching an hour or two of television each week, but you'll probably be able to get by with that small a commitment.

A Goal Minus Commitment

… equals an expectation. When we say goal, we're talking about something to strive toward with a plan to learn and work as much as necessary to achieve it. Expectations, on the other hand, are the source of disappointment. Can we all agree on that? If you expected rich Uncle Clem to leave you ten million dollars and he only left you a million, you'd be disappointed. If you thought he was poor Uncle Clem, didn't expect a cent, and he left you a million dollars, you'd be overjoyed. So the key to contentment lies in your ability to control expectation, not with anything outside of you, like Uncle Clem and his millions.

That's why our strategy for goals is to balance commitment with expectation. It's probably best to get rid of expectation completely, but we're all human, and expectations are a part of life. So one solution is to add an equal amount of commitment. When your commitment and expectation are in line, you have an achievable goal.

Expectation takes you completely out of the present and into the future with no roadmap. There's no declaration of what you're going to do, just an outcome you want. A goal gives you a map. It's a statement. *I am going to do this in order to produce that.* If you can make something happen without any effort from an outside force, you've just broken the laws of physics, you will probably be the most celebrated thinker of all time—and you've just saved us all a ton of gas money.

Eating a Mountain of Jell-O

For those of us who have yet to bring free energy to the world, it might be a good idea to make a goal if we want to accomplish something. So if you're on board with that, we've got something else that you might want to try.

One big, long-term goal is fine, but it can get overwhelming. If you find yourself staring at that mountain of Jell-O, just think "one bite at a time." As part of your roadmap, set coordinated, short-term goals that are very achievable. Here's an example: *I'm going to master right-to-left targets at 25 yards. I'm going to take one hour, three days a week and shoot nothing but right-to-lefts until breaking them doesn't feel any more challenging than tying my shoe. Then I'll move on to left-to-rights.* You see how this smaller goal also serves as a commitment?

There are thousands of goals like that, and we're not going to name them all, but we will talk in general about the types of goals that have proved beneficial for our students. For beginners, goals that have to do with mastering a certain target presentation are very effective, as are goals focused around practicing the move, such as a goal to do the flashlight exercise once a day, mounting the gun 50 times. Intermediate and advanced shooters should still do these types of things, but they have done them so many times as beginners that they shouldn't have to tell themselves to practice their gun mount at home every night or to focus on their weakest target presentations. These things should be part of their routine.

In our experience, intermediate and advanced shooters have tremendous success when they begin setting short-term goals that are based on the mental game, things like refining focus and enhancing feel. As they progress, if their goals become less outcome-oriented and more process oriented, they find consistency faster than they do when they simply focus on results, such as beating a specific person or shooting a certain score. A fellow Level III instructor and student by the name of Brian Brewton gave an interesting example on the "Coaching Hour." Brian said that his performance was really enhanced when he set the goal to make what he calls "the trinity" – focus, feel and trust – a part of every practice session. In other words, every time he picked up the shotgun, he was reminding himself that he wouldn't reach the next level thinking solely about mechanics. He knew that "the trinity" allowed him to enter the zone more easily, and if he could walk into and out of the zone in practice, chances are it would happen more consistently in competition.

Other good examples of process-oriented goals might include setting aside three hours each week to ingrain your pre-shot routine; truly committing to writing in your shooting log *every* time you play with your gun; or shooting 20 targets, real or imaginary, each day without allowing yourself a single mechanical thought.

Dean Olson, another very consistent shooter we've had the pleasure of coaching, says he is at his best when he simply sets a yearly goal of keeping his family, business, and shooting life balanced. Now, he still has other goals, and he still goes into every tournament trusting that he's got what it takes to win, but he's discovered a secret that a lot of other good shooters overlook: If you're focused and calm in other parts of your life, you're more likely to be focused and calm in a shotgun stand. Very few people take the principles of peak performance home from the sporting clays range and apply them to other aspects of their lives, and they're short-changing themselves if they don't. Trying to change unproductive behavior on the range while keeping the same bad habits in other parts of your life is like eating a half-gallon of Blue Bell ice cream six days a week and then expecting to lose weight because you only eat salad on Sundays.

Marry a Goal, Set a Boundary

For most people, once they set a serious goal and make the commitment to achieve it, they tend to think it's carved in granite. Man, they're gonna reach that goal, come hell or high water, and they will accept nothing less. There will be no deviation from the timeline. They have imagined the exact path that's going to get them there. And then life happens.

Please, please, please—be flexible with your goals and forgive yourself if you don't achieve them. Determination is a fine thing and it plays a huge role in sticking to commitments, but having too much of it can block out reality. Once you make your goal and write it down in your log, it's okay to change it. It's okay to change it after the first week, it's okay to change it after the first month, the third month, or anytime down the road. It's okay to change it based on whatever is going on in your life. There's a difference between being firm with your commitments and being afraid to change them. If they need to change, change them. Honor the new commitments and forget the old ones. Maybe you sold your house and moved, took on a new business venture, or just had a new addition to your family. These things tend to have an impact on your time. When they happen and affect your commitments, don't be afraid to change your goals. The same also goes for making bigger goals and increasing commitment. If you want to set a bigger goal and make a deeper commitment once you start down the path, go ahead; just try to be realistic with how much time will be required.

When you get married to a goal, it almost immediately turns into an expectation. This will eventually become your boundary because you can't get past it in your mind. We see this a lot—shooters who won't change a goal even though their circumstances are different, and when that happens, the goal becomes an expectation, producing disappointment, frustration, blame, and judgment. We'll talk more about where all those emotions go, but you can probably guess that it's not to a happy ending.

What's Next?

Would you like to know why it doesn't really matter whether you fail or succeed in your goals? Because the next step should always be the same: setting a new goal. If you have success, you should enjoy it and set a new goal. If you fail, you should learn from it and set a new goal. The only difference is that you always learn more from a failure.

The only problem with failure comes from your reaction to it. Like our old buddy Bob "Snowflake" Shannon has remarked on the "Coaching Hour," you've got to forgive yourself for not achieving a goal. If you don't, you won't learn a damn thing. Accept it, forgive it, and do the same thing you would do if you had succeeded: move on.

Regardless of success or failure, it's very important to set a new goal. Maybe it's the same goal, bigger or smaller than the one before, but we've found that students who don't set new goals tend to flounder. That's because goals guide your idle thought process, and we can probably all admit that our idle thoughts need some guidance. The more you think about something and give emotion to it, the more it becomes you.

In essence, a goal is just something that helps you become the person you choose to be. It helps you make the right decisions, directing you toward something. But remember that the ultimate goal is simply personal. A specific goal you set for yourself is just encouragement toward optimum performance. It's simply leading you through your journey of learning, enjoyment and enlightenment. It's a reminder. When you have a specific, committed goal, it's much easier to make that decision to go out there and practice when it's raining, because you'll end up shooting in the rain eventually.

Here's one last word on goals. Actually, one last phrase: you've gotta believe. We'll go out on a limb and say that most people don't make the necessary commitments to their goals because they don't really believe they can accomplish them. That's why the "what are you going to give up?" question is so tricky. Giving up something is a good sign that you really believe in your goal.

So you can set any goal you want, but if you don't absolutely believe in your heart of hearts that you can achieve it, there's no point in having it. And there are two ways to go about that: either set little goals or have a big belief in yourself.

Do you even need to ask which one we'd pick?

Craig Hill on Commitment

Craig Hill is an elite sporting clays shooter, a student, and friend of ours. Craig has achieved many of his goals, one being to make the All-American Team. A short while after Craig received his All-American shooting vest from the NSCA, he talked to us about his difficulty in setting a new goal and the commitment it would take to achieve it.

For Craig, setting the ultimate goal of becoming world champion was a logical next step for him, but a difficult one in light of the huge commitment it would take. He said, "I'm in my early forties, I've developed the talent to go there, and I've got the resources and time to do it, but I also know just how much it will take for me to do it."

After years of experience, he knew that to be at the top of his game, he would need to have an intense training practice session three times a week. That may not sound like a lot until you look at it on a calendar. All told, including travel time to and from the club, each one of these sessions would take four or five hours out of his day. That's about a half a day, three days a week. He also knew he would have to train with a coach every two or three weeks, watch his diet, go to the gym for physical conditioning, and shoot at least 10 out-of-town major shoots, plus the U.S. Open, his state shoot, zone shoot, and the Nationals. All told, that meant devoting around 16 hours a week to training and practice, plus giving up 14 weekends for tournaments. If you want to be world champion, prepare yourself for this type of commitment.

Chapter Recap

- Consistency is a result of commitment.

- A goal is a commitment. Write down your goals and write down what you are going to give up to achieve them.

- Expectations are the cause of disappointment. If you can learn to balance your expectations with commitment, you'll learn to conquer this.

- Set smaller, more achievable goals as a roadmap to larger goals.

- Setting more process-oriented goals that have to do with the mental game has been very successful for our students. This includes goals such as refining focus and writing in a log every day.

- Be flexible with your goals and forgiving with yourself if you don't achieve them. It's okay to change a goal at any time, especially if your commitment changes.

- Always set a new goal, regardless of whether you fail or succeed in an old goal.

- A goal is worthless unless you truly believe in it.

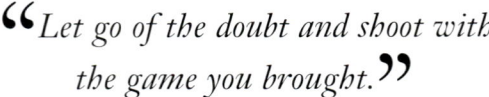

"Let go of the doubt and shoot with the game you brought."

CHAPTER FOUR

The FEEL BLOCKER

The toothless dog. The old wicked one. Conscious doubt. These are some of the names that have been given to what we call "the voice." Add "feel blocker" to that list, because that's exactly what it can do. But if you can get to know the voice, learn how to deal with it, and direct it in a way that allows feel to dominate, you have developed one of the most important skills in shotgun sports—and life, too, in our opinion. This is the key to the next level, folks—it's like the dough for your consistency pie.

Our charge to the beginning shooter is to get a firm grasp on each of the six trajectories and ingrain the move and mount through practice. But for intermediate and advanced shooters, we add voice mastery to the mix. Yes, more advanced shooters will always be working on fundamentals, refining them to higher and higher levels, but consistency will be much harder won if they can't control the voice. It doesn't matter if you've got the best move and mount in the world; if your thoughts distract you from focus, you might as well be spitting at the target.

We touched on this in *If It Ain't Broke*, but for those who aren't familiar with it or need a quick refresher, when we talk about the voice, we're referring to the non-stop burbling of thoughts that goes on in your head, specifically those that are judgmental. We call it the voice of conscious doubt, Inner Game guru Tim Gallwey calls it Self One, and we're sure there are a million other names it's been given. What does it say? It takes just about any form you can imagine, but in sporting clays, common phrases include things like: *Teal always give me trouble. I'm just not good at shooting them. I didn't get enough sleep last night. How am I going to hit anything in this wind? I can't concentrate when I'm in the stand and that lady keeps talking. Why did they have to put me on a squad with this idiot? This course is really hard. I'm not as good as these guys. I don't belong here.*

Okay, those are obvious. They're negative thoughts, and we all know we should think positively, but this is about much more than positive thinking. The voice will take on many different personas. Here's one that surprises a lot of people: *This stand is easy; it'll be a cakewalk.* At first glance, that's a positive thought, but it's really the voice making a judgment and lulling you into a false sense of security. If you listen to it, you won't give the targets the respect they deserve. When you don't respect a target, you don't focus well, and when you don't focus well, you miss.

That one also shows how the voice tends to take you out of the present. Does this sound familiar? *I've only missed eight targets with two stations left. If I run these out I'll finally break 90 and win this shoot.* Or how about this? *I've already dropped 10 targets and I'm only through three stations. I'm on my way to a terrible score.* When the voice is saying stuff like this, you are in the future. You've already decided the outcome in your head. If you believe the voice in either situation, it'll always sabotage your performance.

Another thing the voice likes to do is talk mechanics. It'll pipe up during competition and tell you that you're holding the gun way too high or way too low, or your feet aren't set right, or that you need to measure the lead. Mechanics have their place during practice when you're refining your move, but if you let mechanical thoughts dominate during competition, tapping into feel and entering the zone is out of the question. Just the fact that you're constantly reminding yourself of swing mechanics means you doubt them. The fact that you're thinking about lead means you doubt your subconscious ability to put the gun where it needs to be. Let go of the doubt and shoot with the game you brought. You're either letting feel dominate or letting thought dominate, not both at the same time.

And finally, if it sounds like a five year-old throwing a temper tantrum, it's probably the voice. If it sounds like a nagging parent, it's probably the voice. If it's jabbering at you like it's your pimp, then it's definitely the voice. The way we all talk to ourselves can be pretty amazing. *You dumb sonuvabitch, can't you keep your *#&@! eyes still before you call pull? You're pathetic, the target's only twenty yards away, everybody else hit it, and you can't cornflake it to save your life. Why are you playing a game you suck at?* We wouldn't let anybody in the world treat us like this and get away with it, but we do it to ourselves without batting an eye.

Going Mental

Most people would say that getting a handle on the voice is the "mental game," and we agree, but we think you'll be surprised that some of the techniques we're going to outline are fairly physical. We're also careful of calling it the mental game, because the common notion seems to be that you don't really need to practice the mental game. Once you understand it, you've got it. That is a big, steaming pile in our opinion, and if you don't think you need to practice the "mental game," you might as well stop reading right now.

Our method depends on changing behavior on and off the field, like we talked about in the last chapter. It has to work that way, because the voice only talks about the things that you feed it. If you don't put it in your head, the voice won't talk about it. It will only run with the subjects you give it. If you look at nudie magazines all day, the voice is going to talk about nudie magazines. Indulge the doubt voice in your personal life, and there's little chance you'll get rid of it on a sporting clays course. But if you are consumed with mastering the voice and fostering inner stillness while in the stand, the voice will even talk about that.

It's a mistake to think of this as self-deception, because it's only deception if you try to do it for a few hours once in a while. What we're talking about is self-direction on a constant basis. Because, in the words of our buddy Homer Saye, "If your head ain't right, your ass can't follow."

> **The Science Behind It**
> *There is scientific evidence to back up our practice of turning the shot over to the subconscious mind. It has been documented that people respond two-tenths of a second faster to visuals than they do to verbal commands. Scientists have asked subjects to react to a verbal command of "stop!" versus reacting to a red light. They always respond faster to the red light by an average of two-tenths of a second. So if you can turn your shot over to the part of your brain that uses pictures instead of words, you've already improved your reaction time to the target.*

Chapter Recap

- The voice is the internal monologue that's constantly going on in your mind.

- The voice blocks feel by scattering your focus over many different thoughts that often conflict with your goal.

- Learning how to deal with the voice and direct it is a big key to consistency.

- The voice tends to favor judgmental, negative thoughts, and it loves to talk about mechanics and lead, but it can also come in other forms, like overconfidence.

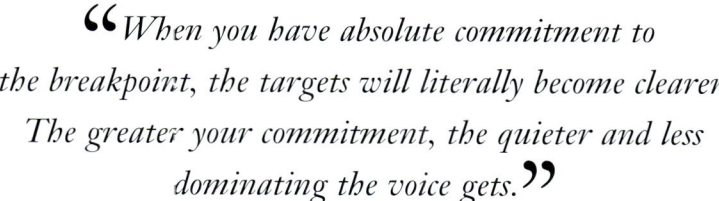

"When you have absolute commitment to the breakpoint, the targets will literally become clearer. The greater your commitment, the quieter and less dominating the voice gets."

CHAPTER FIVE

VOICE MANAGEMENT

Have you ever looked at your dog or cat and received that completely blank stare in return? You get the same thing from brand-new babies. It's a look you rarely see from adults unless they're *lost in concentration*. We'd venture to say that's the look of a mind dominated by the subconscious. It's instinct driven. A voiceless look. That's what we want you to have when you're in the stand—and we promise not to comment about the drool or dirty diapers.

Does Awareness Sound Familiar?

Before you become a drill sergeant with yourself or start pounding on your head, just take some time to observe what your voice says in different situations. Let it say what it wants when you miss a target or run a stand. Everyone will have a unique voice, and before you try to manage yours, you should get to know it. Jot down some of the things it tends to say. Is it the "oh no" voice or the "oh boy" voice? Does it beat you up or puff you up? In our experience, as you get better, the voice tends to take on things that sound good or positive, even though they mask doubt or take you out of the present. It's even more clever than you are, and it's so sneaky that most of us rarely pay attention to what it's saying. But if you can't recognize the voice, you can do nothing to control it.

You should also listen to some of the things other shooters say about themselves. We guarantee that you could go to a shooting range right now—or to a golf course, tennis or basketball court, or anywhere else people are playing sports or performing—and find at least one example of someone being controlled by the voice of conscious doubt. We see it over and over again when students miss, especially in front of several others. They want to let you know they're better than that, so they curse at themselves or make a big show when the targets aren't breaking. We've all been there, where the first priority is to look good or avoid embarrassment, and focus on the actual target comes in a distant second place … or tenth place, for that matter.

So listen to the parking lot chatter after a tournament or a friendly round, and you'll hear the voice loud and clear. Pay attention to what happens to your own thoughts when someone else is letting the voice out. Does it make your negative voice stronger when your buddy is whining about the weather or the course or what a shitty day he had? Just be aware of it for a while, without worrying about making any big changes.

Put Him to Work
Once you're sensitive to the voice and the type of things he says to you, it'll be much easier to understand what it feels like when you put him in the backseat. Erasing all thoughts from your head for long periods of time is a great concept, and there are probably a few elite performers who can do it consistently, but

we like to start our students with a slightly smaller challenge. The goal we set is to take the reins from the thought-oriented, conscious mind and give them to the feel-oriented subconscious for a few seconds at a time when you're in the stand. To do that, we recommend putting the voice to work. Give your conscious mind something helpful to focus on that becomes a clear signal: it's time to trust the subconscious. Commitment to the breakpoint is the most effective signal we've found.

This will sound familiar if you've read any of our material before, but we don't mind repeating ourselves. The breakpoint is a very specific, predetermined spot where you've decided you will break the target once you see its flight path. It's as simple as saying, "I will pull the trigger when the clay reaches that tree (or whatever point you pick)." When you do that, the breakpoint becomes the true target, and you merge with the clay in that predetermined spot and pull the trigger. In picking a breakpoint, you're putting your analytical voice to work, tying it up with that task.

Did We Mention Commitment?

A big part of coaching is saying the same thing over and over in different ways until it finally sinks in, and we're going to do that here. To effectively occupy the voice, your commitment to the breakpoint must be ironclad. We've referred to it as the commitment of a skydiver. When a skydiver jumps, that boy is committed to pulling the ripcord, and he's got a certain window in which to do it. As a shooter, your window is the breakpoint. When you feel your muzzles merge ahead of the target in that breakpoint, ***pull the trigger***.

It's a matter of eliminating all other thoughts through your commitment to the breakpoint. The strength of that commitment determines how much focus you have and how strong it is. You can't be any more focused than you are committed. When you have absolute commitment to the breakpoint, the targets will literally become clearer. The greater your commitment, the quieter and less dominating the voice gets. We've illustrated this by setting up a rabbit target and asking students to shoot it between two markers. They'll usually pull the trigger at the last moment, when the target has nearly passed the second marker. Then somebody like Don Yost, who brought this up on the "Coaching Hour" will realize that the delay is happening because of a soft commitment. Don had been shooting for over ten years, but he said the exercise helped him realize that he was still letting the conscious mind measure the lead, instead of trusting and pulling the trigger.

"It was frightening to realize how many times I thought I was not measuring when in fact there was just that fractional second when I made double sure," Don says. "It just dawned on me that the only way [to break them early] was to just plan on pulling the trigger, period, when it was time to pull it in that zone. And the targets were breaking, and I began to apply that to everything."

When you check the barrel and measure lead, you take your eyes off the target. When you trust your plan and commit to a breakpoint, you tie up the voice and enhance your focus. If your plan is weak or confused, your focus is gone. If instead of focusing on the target at hand, you're thinking about the guy who cut you off on the freeway, how you just ran the last stand, or the embarrassment of missing the last two pairs, it's over.

So it's more important to be decisive with the breakpoint than correct. If you're decisive with it and you're wrong, it's very obvious that you picked the wrong place. If not, it's less obvious, and it will be hard to tell if you missed because of focus or

> **Method For Our Madness**
>
> *For the unfamiliar, the method we advocate for almost all situations involves keeping the gun in front of the target (what some call "maintained lead"), swinging the gun the same speed as the target, never looking at the barrel, and merging ahead of the target at the breakpoint, as if you were merging into a break in traffic on the freeway.*
>
> *After all, the gun must be in the breakpoint before the target arrives in order to be ahead of the target. If you try to be "on time", you will be late and miss behind. It's okay to be in the breakpoint early because the only two options you have are early or late. When you are early, the feeling is here it comes. When you are late, the feeling is there it goes.*
>
> *It is much easier to be early in the breakpoint and catch the target as it comes than to try to be on time, ending up late and having to chase it. When you are early in the breakpoint, the lead is already there. It's okay to be early. How early? Don't worry about it. Trust your subconscious. It knows how early if you are truly focused on the front of the target. We have found that it's more important to be precise with focus than with lead. For more details, please refer to Chapters 3, 6, 7, 8, 11, and 19 of* If It Ain't Broke, Fix It!

because of your plan. Commit to your plan. If it's right, duplicate it; if not, change it.

Stevie Ray's Swing Thoughts

We've talked about Steve Brown (The East Texas Gentleman) before, and while he's had a tremendous influence on all of our teachings, this next part is especially owed to him. Stevie Ray is a wonderful friend and a highly-gifted Level III instructor at Prairie Creek Sporting Clays near Tyler, Texas. If you get the chance to go study with him, you're a damned fool if you don't.

Stevie Ray's take on the voice is this: completely silencing your thoughts just ain't gonna happen when you are in a pressure situation. As he puts it, "You can't 'silence the lambs,' not when the terms are important to you."

If it's your first time in the U.S. Open, that voice is going to be gnawing on your ear. So in addition to tying up the voice in the breakpoint, Steve suggests occupying the voice with feel-oriented swing thoughts.

This is Stevie Ray's mantra in the stand, once he has picked his breakpoints and committed to them. "I tell myself: 'ready.' That's the point where I go to my voice," he says. "I let my voice say this: 'I feel my front hand moving to where the target is headed, gradually letting the target overtake me.' " When he merges with the target at the breakpoint, Steve has his voice yell, **"Three O' Clock!"** or whatever position of the clock matches the front edge of the target. If it's a right-to-left crosser, he would use nine o' clock, a dropping teal, six o' clock. Even though he's focused on the target the entire time, this gives him a visually-oriented command to focus intensely on the front edge of the target as he pulls the trigger.

"Now, between shots or while I'm loading my gun, you don't think my voice is running crazy?" Steve says. "But all you have to do is give it something to do for a couple of seconds. I haven't tried this yet, but I think I could let you put my big toe in a vise and squeeze on it a little bit, and I believe I could think about Sharon Stone or Demi Moore and block everything out for about three seconds."

We're not asking you to put any of your appendages in a vise, but it's a good idea to play with different swing thoughts to see what works best for you. We'd suggest using those that give you a strong visual, such as a clock face. If you think you can completely silence the voice with the sheer power of your focus, try that, too. What works best will vary from person to person.

Whatever You Do, Don't

At this point, we'd like to ask you, please, don't picture a cow's ass. When you're done not picturing that, try not to think about the Pope in his underwear. And make sure you don't think about little green men humping your leg. Have you successfully not pictured any of those things?

Okay, you probably get the point of this nonsense: If we ask you not to think about something, you're going to think it. If we ask you not to picture something, you're going to picture it. For the most part, you can keep your body from doing something by using the word "don't," but you can't expect to keep your mind off something by telling yourself not to think it. Your subconscious doesn't understand the word "don't." The instant you name an image, your subconscious will call it up, even if "don't think about" is in front of it.

> **Guided by a Weiner:**
> *The eyes are like the hands' seeing-eye dog. And when you get up there and you let the voice go rampant, the eyes go with it, and you might as well have somebody giving you a six-month-old weenie dog. It's not going to work. You're going to get run over in traffic.*
> —Steve

That's why, in managing your voice, it might not be effective to use repression as a strategy. Some of our students say they've had success controlling the voice by talking to themselves firmly when they hear it, but it doesn't involve the word "don't." Tom Kirchmer says this: "I've learned my voice doesn't like confrontation. So I start doing it when I'm shooting, once in a while it'll creep in. I just kind of learned to say, 'Just shut the you-know-what up.' And it goes away. My voice doesn't like that."

Now, maybe that works for Tom because he's telling it to do something, "shut the bleep up," rather than asking it **not** to do something. Dick Baker tells us that a similar form of self-talk works for him. "I've gone by several names," Dick says, "but I had an old Marine friend; when he called me Richard, god damn, things were serious. And I want to tell you, when I say 'Richard' and talk to it ... if you really want to get rid of the voice, pick out what your mother always called you."

If calling himself Richard works for him, we're all for it, but we hope he avoids making statements like, "Richard, don't think about the wind, don't think about your score, don't think about the fact that you're in the lead."

Using phrases like these is using one form of the voice to talk to another, because these are actually statements of doubt, which confuses your subconscious. The response to "don't think about the wind" is *why not? Is wind a problem? What happened the last time I shot in the wind?* The same goes for the others. Your subconscious searches your memory for the things that happened the last time you thought about score or thought about being in the lead, and it calls those things to mind.

Laughing at the Jester

Another strategy that's been effective for students, courtesy of Stevie Ray, is to actually accept and encourage the voice. When you're approaching a big shooting challenge or whenever the voice is particularly loud, Steve says to "anxiously await what will come into your head next." Let the voice be your jester. See just how ridiculous your thoughts can be.

One example is Willy Cherry. When the voice is chewing on him, he tells himself, "Okay, I'm starting to think crazy thoughts, and I wonder how crazy they're going to get. And I just sit back and kind of wait for them and see how silly and ridiculous they can be. And then step into the box and go: 'Okay, I'm going to shoot these now and come back in a minute or two and see if I can think of something even more ridiculous than that.'"

This technique allows Willy to give less credibility and less emotion to the voice instead of getting frustrated. It won't keep the voice from getting in, but you might be surprised how fast it gets out of your way, how short-lived it becomes when you ask it to perform. You can then get on with your helpful, positive, action-oriented thoughts.

Mind Matters

Different people will have different voices and their own preferred method of managing them. But while looking for your own, keep in mind the goal behind all this, which is to turn your swing over to the subconscious, instinctive part of yourself—the part that feels. In order to find the most effective way of managing the conscious mind and speaking to the subconscious, we've found it helpful to breakdown the attributes of each.

The conscious mind is the mind you analyze with. It's the thinker. It makes decisions and judges the result. Without it, there would be no voice. You have to use it every time you set up for a target; it's the one that makes the plan. It also has tremendous short-term memory. It carries the same misses from station to station and obsesses over things that have just happened. The conscious mind understands words; in fact, words are its treasured possession. It responds to the language of logic. It gives commands, but it is not tied directly to movement, and so it is not tied directly to your swing.

The subconscious mind is the one that operates below conscious awareness. It's the feeler. It does things without the conscious mind even knowing about it. It's not logical and does not understand logic. It's physical and emotional. It cannot think; it can only feel. When you're doing something without thought, the subconscious mind is involved. The language it uses is the language of pictures, not words. It is also the home of instinct and intuition. It does not make decisions. It only responds. What does it respond to? It receives instructions from the conscious mind and carries them out in a very literal way. **When your conscious mind produces a thought, your subconscious mind works 100 percent of its available time to bring about what you thought.** The instant you say it or think it, the subconscious goes to work. With proper instructions, it will direct the body to do what you've trained it to do, and it will do that most effectively without interference from the conscious mind. It doesn't question or analyze. All it does is wait: it's sittin' in the chair, waiting to do something.

The subconscious mind has a huge storehouse of long-term memory. Everything that you've ever done is in your subconscious. Every great shot you've ever made is waiting there, ready to be recalled. Every bad shot you've ever made, every poor performance you've ever made is waiting there to be recalled. The thoughts you give it determine which one it picks.

Friend or Foe?

We've said before that the voice is not your friend once you step into a stand, but it might not be effective to think of him as your enemy either. The best advice might be to use the best tool for the task. Let the conscious mind analyze the target presentation and plan the shot. This can be the voice's territory. But when it comes to feel, do whatever is necessary to keep the voice from being dominant. This is the time for your subconscious. Once you have trained your move so many times that it will happen without thinking, do you really need to think about it?

The conscious mind and the voice are not your enemies, but they are not connected directly to your swing, so they aren't the best tools for that task. The conscious mind thinks it is, and our culture is very conscious mind-oriented, so we've given it a lot of exercise while neglecting the feely subconscious. When was the last time you heard of a teacher telling students to access the non-logical mind?

But the conscious mind produces the voice, and the voice obscures feel. When it is dominant, you are thinking, not feeling. You are not instinctive. You are reacting to your own thoughts instead of what's happening around you. That's all it is when we talk about choking under pressure. Someone who chokes is simply so distracted by their thoughts that they're unable to perform something that is normally easy for them.

We've said this many times: Until every shot is a 100 percent felt reaction to the target, you have room to improve. And keep in mind that giving the subconscious control of the swing doesn't guarantee a break. You can still make an error in planning the shot or lose sight of the target behind the barrel, but we can guarantee that you will miss less often and better understand the reason you missed if you use the right tool for the task.

Chapter Recap

- If you want a good example of a "voiceless face," have a look at a newborn baby or someone lost in concentration.

- In order to control the voice, you must first recognize it. Take some time to simply pay attention to your thoughts, to what the voice likes to say to you.

- Putting the voice to work is an effective way to let the subconscious take over. We do this by tying the voice up with the breakpoint.

- Feel-oriented swing thoughts can also tie up the voice.

Vinny's Voices

Our travels took us to Georgia where we met Vincent Hancock, an interesting kid who had just trained with the Olympic International Skeet Team. Well, he'd not only trained with them, he'd beaten them all in International Skeet—at age 15. When we found that out, Gil asked him to tell us about his voices, if they were silent. Vinny said, "No, sir, Mr. Ash, my voices were agreeing."

Gil said, "Really?"

"Yes sir," Vinny replied. "They were both agreed on the fact that I was going to hit that bird."

We'd never heard it put that way, but it's an interesting way to phrase what we're talking about. Eventually all the voices in your internal conversation are going to agree. They're either going to agree that you're going to smash the target in the breakpoint, or they're going to agree that you can't hit the bird. And until you can turn all those voices into one voice through focus and a commitment to the breakpoint, they're going to create confusion, hesitation, and frustration.

- Picking a breakpoint is good, but committing 100 percent to a breakpoint is better.

- Repression of thoughts is not an effective strategy. Telling yourself ***not*** to think about something is self-defeating.

- Some students have had success treating the voice like a jester. Let it entertain you. The conscious mind is not your enemy, it's just not the best tool for the task when taking the shot.

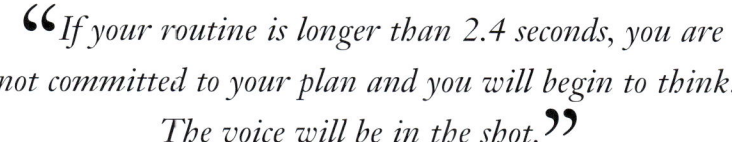

> *"If your routine is longer than 2.4 seconds, you are not committed to your plan and you will begin to think. The voice will be in the shot."*

CHAPTER SIX

The PRE-SHOT ROUTINE

The subconscious knows rhythm. For those of you who can clap a steady rhythm without music, do you consciously think about when you're going to clap next? Do you tick off the seconds in your head? No, you just feel the rhythm.

Using that rhythm to manage the voice and stimulate feel is what the pre-shot routine is all about. It's a crucial part of turning your swing over to the subconscious. If you'll think back to elementary school music class, though, you'll remember the teacher asking you to tick off numbers in order to learn rhythm. One and two and three and four. It always starts with the conscious mind, and the pre-shot routine is no different.

A Routine Template
After you've entered the cage, asked the trapper questions about the targets, and watched the view pair all the way to the ground, you'll want to have a consistent routine. Here's an example of

the basic pre-shot routine we teach: I confirm my plan because picking a breakpoint for each of the birds should be the first thing I do. **I then load the shells** into the gun, rest it on the rail, and with my left hand (or right hand if I'm a lefty), I point at breakpoint one. As I do that, I tell myself, "I'm going to break the first one there," and visualize the target exploding.

I then move my hand to breakpoint two and repeat the same thing. I come back to the first breakpoint and focus hard on that spot. **As I close the gun**, I shift focus to the focal point (the place where I will first see the bird), and address the target by placing the gun in the hold point.

My eyes are in that focal point like a laser, and within 2.4 seconds from the time I close the gun, I call pull. Boom, boom, and the shot is over.

The Cue and the Trigger

The two phrases in bold above are important because they represent the cue and the trigger. For us, loading the gun is the cue to begin. When you load that gun (or whatever cue you choose), the door should close behind you, and from then on your routine should be the same every time. At this point, it's okay to stare at that first breakpoint long enough to commit to that spot and have 100 percent belief that you'll break it there. This should bring the voice's volume way down. If the target seems particularly stout to you, or when you are in a situation where the voice might be particularly loud, you may want to do just that. Take an extra long time at that first breakpoint after you load the gun. But you should maintain consistency in the steps: breakpoint one, breakpoint two, back to breakpoint one. So the cue is just a signal that it's time to get in your bubble and turn your many voices into one voice, focused on the breakpoints.

After the cue to begin, when you are in your bubble, you still need to use the conscious mind (the voice) to plan the shot and pick the breakpoints.

The trigger is a physical action that you perform when you have confirmed your plan and are ready to shoot the pair. The trigger can be anything: a deep breath, closing the gun, squeezing the gun lightly, or shifting weight, but it must be something. It will be a signal to your brain to turn off conscious planning and release subconscious function. Like a light switch. We use closing the gun, but again, it can be anything.

After the trigger, the timing is very important. Between 1.4 and 2.4 seconds after the trigger, we want our students calling pull, and we want that rhythm to be the same every time. By that we mean the same amount of time between **close ... address ... pull**. That rhythm is personal, but it should always be the same, and it should take less than two and a half seconds. The rhythm should not be close ... address ... ... pull, nor should it be close ... ... address ... pull. It should be a consistent rhythm with a defined beat.

And why the timing between 1.4 and 2.4 seconds? If your routine is less than 1.4 seconds, there is a good chance that your eyes will be moving and your body tense, instead of still and relaxed, when you call pull. If your routine is longer than 2.4 seconds, you are not committed to your plan and you will begin to think. The voice will be in the shot.

It's okay to be conscious of this time limit and your rhythm in the beginning. Once it's an established rhythm, you won't have to think about it.

The trigger is the point of no return. It's like a light switch that turns off conscious planning and releases subconscious action. After the trigger, if you are distracted, hesitant, or pulled out of focus in any way, break the gun and start the routine over. Let us repeat that because so many people find it difficult to do.

Break the gun and start the routine over. If thoughts of score creep in, break the gun and start over. If someone on your squad distracts you, break the gun and start over. If the target comes out broken, start the routine over. If you suddenly start thinking about what you're going to cook for dinner, do we have to tell you what to do, or have you picked up on the rhythm?

Making It Yours

If you don't have a pre-shot routine, try the template we suggested and see how it feels. There's definitely flexibility to use a different sequence, a different cue or a different trigger, and most of our students do something slightly different. If you want to take a slow, deep breath that ends as you perform your trigger, do that, but do it every time. Whatever your final routine is, just remember a few things:

- It should be the same every time. Your cue and trigger should be the same. Like we said, the preamble after the cue and before the trigger where you're pointing at breakpoints is more flexible time-wise. At this point, you are acquiring focus and relaxed concentration (relaxed body, focused mind). But once you perform your trigger, everything should be exactly the same. This is when your focus should be locked on, and you should feel a powerful inner stillness.
- Always visit the first breakpoint last. The reason we want you to do this is because the subconscious works on thought inventory: last in, first out. The last thing you visualize and burn into your brain before your trigger is the first place your body will want to go.
- Incorporate visualization and movement. In the beginning, we like students to point at the breakpoints because it engages feel through movement. We like them to visualize both birds exploding in the breakpoints because it engages

the subconscious through mental pictures.

- Keep it simple. Most of us confuse the subconscious by giving it too many commands. It needs no more instruction than "breakpoint one, breakpoint two." This is a simple, solution-oriented command. The challenge is breaking the targets; the solution is in the breakpoints. If you let the voice dominate, it will say things like, *I've got to have these to win. I don't want to embarrass myself. Focus on the target. Keep your stance right. Relax your hands. I can't shoot with that noise in the background.* And it will say these things within the span of a few seconds. The subconscious can't compute all of these things at once, and it won't.

Pheasant Routine?
Does this routine thing really work? Ask Jack Parker. He's a student who's had the routine work so well for him in sporting clays that he joked about wanting to find some kind of routine for live birds, too. "After missing quite a few pheasants in South Dakota, I started trying to call pull as they flushed," Jack said. "It didn't work."

- Try matching the rhythm after the cue to the rhythm of the target presentation. Here's what we mean: Let's say you're shooting a lightning fast crossing target, followed by a very slow teal going up. Because you want the speed of your move to match the speed of the target, you'll want to move fast on the crosser and very slowly on the teal. So it just makes sense to imbed this rhythm while you're pointing at the breakpoints. See it, break it ... see it ... ... break it. Point quickly at the first breakpoint, slowly at the second. Each stand has a rhythm and you can work that into your plan. Vicki has helped a lot of students with this, and the results are impressive. Remember, always visit the first breakpoint last!

- Jot down your preferred routine in your log. In the beginning, this will help you remember exactly what you decided on. It will probably evolve over time, but this gives you a starting point for that evolution.
- Use it! This seems obvious, but so does using shampoo, and yet they still have to put the directions on the bottle. For those of you who would be walking around with a head full of soap without them, let us make it plain: use the pre-shot routine every time you visit the clays range. Whether you're shooting singles or pairs, every shot should be taken with a routine.
- For a visual walk-through of the basic pre-shot routine, take a look at our new DVD, *Sporting Clays Pre-shot Routine*. It's the most comprehensive DVD on sporting clays routines that we've seen.

Turning It On and Off

We all have limited reserves of intense concentration in each given day. It's like a time bank that seems to be around 30 or 45 minutes with the proper sleep and nutrition. One of the biggest benefits of a routine is that it helps make efficient use of this time. Our friend Nathan Pakish thinks of it as a light switch, and that's a description as good as "entering the bubble" or "shutting the door." When you step into the cage and perform your cue to start the routine, it's like you're switching on that peak concentration meter. When you step out of the cage, you turn it off, which helps to keep from wasting it.

Easy for Us to Say

It's one thing to sit here and write this or read it, but it's a different deal to actually create a routine that is so habitual you don't have to think about it. We understand the challenge of maintaining a routine on every shot for 50 to 100 shots, especially in a competition setting. At first, some of our students find they abandon their routines after a few stands and don't even realize it. This is normal. We also find that our students, while training their routine, miss targets they would normally hit. This is also normal. We understand that you will be consciously aware of it while you're making it a habit, but we promise that it will stick better the more you use it in practice. It's not a bad idea to make a goal of shooting a certain number of stands with a perfect routine.

Training the routine is just like training the move. A strategy of acceptance, like we advocated for managing the voice, might also work here. When teaching beginners, we tell them to accept mechanical thoughts. Trying to fight mechanical thoughts when you're just learning a move and mount doesn't work. You will be mechanical for a while, and the same goes for pre-shot routine. You will think swing mechanics during practice, but you don't want your mind on those things once you have the move in your subconscious database. On game day, it's detrimental to think about swing mechanics, lead, or how many seconds it's taking you to call pull. You want a still mind. It's your pre-shot routine that links your mechanical game to the still mind. Without a consistent, sound, simple and habitual pre-shot routine, we wouldn't expect to perform well mentally or mechanically. Until your pre-shot routine gets to a level where everything is happening subconsciously, you aren't practicing enough or you aren't practicing the right thing.

Chapter Recap

- The subconscious mind understands rhythm. A pre-shot routine is about using rhythm to silence the voice and stimulate feel.

Mick's Mind

Mick Howell is an elite sporting clays shooter we featured on our "Coaching Hour." Here's a short segment on routine that we pulled from one of our interviews with Mick. Keep in mind, we haven't coached him before; this is all Mick's opinion based on his experience.

Gil: When it's your turn to shoot and you step in the box, what is your routine that you go through mentally before you call pull?

Mick: I have to get all thoughts out of my mind. If I'm thinking about lead, choke—if I'm thinking about anything at all when I call pull—that's going to clutter up and get in the way of everything. So I just wait until I can get totally empty-headed and then just do everything on instinct.

Gil: What about messing with your bullets?

Mick: Sometimes I'll turn them so the writing is the right way up, and people say, "Oh, that doesn't make any difference in the way the bullets shoot." And we all know that, obviously, it doesn't, but it's just something for me to do to occupy my mind while I'm getting the right thoughts, which in my case is no thoughts. And then once I'm pretty much clear and my mind's empty and I don't have any stupid thoughts in my head, then I'll go ahead and call pull.

Gil: But now, once you've played with your bullets and your mind's empty, do you close the gun quickly and call, or do you have a rhythm when you close the gun?

Mick: I like to close the gun pretty slowly and just close it so as I know that it's shut tight, because over the years I've had a few times when the top levers move. And so I just close it so I know everything's locked up, and basically so it's all ready to go, but I don't rush anything. And it depends, some days may be quicker than others. You know, some days you may see me standing in the box for ten, fifteen, twenty seconds, and some days it's two seconds and I'm ready to go. I'll just wait until I'm ready.

- A pre-shot routine should be short and sweet, and include a cue to start and a trigger that means the shot is going to happen within 1.4 to 2.4 seconds.

- Once you have a routine that feels good to you, jot it down in your log so that it doesn't change.

- Use the routine on every shot, every time you shoot, whether that's practice or competition.

- A routine will not be fully effective until it happens without conscious direction, just like your move and mount.

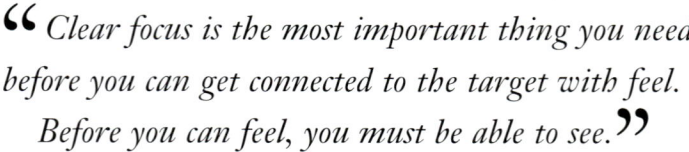

" Clear focus is the most important thing you need before you can get connected to the target with feel. Before you can feel, you must be able to see."

CHAPTER SEVEN

BEFORE YOU CAN FEEL

In all this talk about feel and getting shooty-feely, you might be surprised when we say that there is one thing equally important—maybe more important, because you need to have it before you can connect with the target through feel.

Any guesses?

How about this: If you're an intermediate or advanced shooter, have you ever been locked on a target, super focused, feeling like you had it, but when you pulled the trigger, it didn't break—even though you were so sure you felt connected? In fact, you were on a roll; you were in the zone. The voice was quiet, you were focused, everything seemed perfect. It felt right, man, but it just didn't break, almost like you're shooting blanks. Ready for an answer that is so simple it'll sound ridiculous?

You didn't see the target.

This is where you go, "Huh?"

That's right, you didn't see the target when you pulled the trigger.

Insane, you say? Your eyes were open? You didn't flinch? That may be, but in our experience, when this happens, it's almost always because the gun partially occluded your focus on the target. It may have only occluded it a tiny bit, but that's all it takes. The true cause for the miss is hidden behind the obvious. This is what we call "getting jammed by the bird."

Clear focus is the most important thing you need before you can get connected to the target with feel. Before you can feel, you must be able to see. Maybe if you're related to Luke Skywalker you can wear a blindfold and use The Force, but for the rest of us, an unobstructed view of the target is essential.

Occlusions

Webster defines the word occlusion as *in the way, to shut, to close, to stop up, and to shut in or out*. Keep in mind that in order for your subconscious brain to know where to insert the gun, the eyes must have an unobstructed view of the target **and** the lead. When the target jams the gun or gets inside the lead, the eyes can no longer project ahead what the lead and line are, so the gun has become an occlusion. This is what we call "playing too close to the bird."

Playing too close to the bird with the gun occludes the visual input to the brain, which in turn causes a miss, typically over the target. To understand this, it's necessary to understand how the input from the eyes is converted to physical output by the brain. First the retina of the eye begins to process the visual information of the moving target before it sends it to the brain. As the brain receives it, the interpretation of that data goes through several levels of refinement. It is at that point that the subconscious brain knows the lead and line of the target. As long as the visual input is not interrupted, the hands will know where to put the gun to successfully break the target. Any distortion of or interruption of the information flow to the brain from the eyes will result in a missed target.

As long as the eye has an unobstructed view of the target lead and line, the gun can be inserted into the correct place to intercept the target. If, however, the target closes to within the necessary lead to break the target before the shot is taken, the gun is now in the way of the eyes' ability to project ahead the necessary lead and line to hit the target. The gun is now an occlusion to the visual input to the brain. It is not a total occlusion, but a partial occlusion. Because the occlusion is only partial, everything looks right, but the target does not break and the miss is typically over.

Why would the miss be over the target? The eye has been giving the brain the movement data of the target ever since it had it in focus. The lead was continually updated as the eye tracked the target across the sky. When the target jammed the gun or came within the necessary lead to break the target, the eye could continue reading the lead on the target but could not read the line because the gun was in the way. In the last instant, there was a push to get the gun out of the way and the shot was taken. The eye knew the lead but could not predict the line because the gun created a partial occlusion to the eyes' ability to read the correct line. Had there been a total occlusion of the target by the gun, it would have been very obvious to the shooter because they would have lost all perception of the target, and the gun would have been the predominate object in their vision.

Because the occlusion was only partial, it was much less obvious when it occurred. More often than not, this leads the shooter to the wrong conclusion as to why the target was missed. This partial occlusion manifests itself as a timing problem in shotgunning. When the occlusion is significant, there is typically a flinch or jerk or push with the gun while the shooter pulls the trigger. When there is a minimal occlusion, everything looks right, but the target is missed—and the miss is always off line and typically over.

This is why playing too close to the bird with the muzzle creates misses above the target. Over is ***behind***! An easy way to observe this occlusion in action is to view a target, say, a left-to-right crosser, being aware of the line. Watch it from the trap to the ground. Notice how obvious the line is on the target. Watch several targets. Then call for a target and follow it just in front with your index finger, keeping the target and your finger close together. You will immediately see the occlusion and feel how you want to do anything you can to get your finger out of the way so you can see the line. You can instantly see how difficult it becomes to easily distinguish the line of the target when the target gets too close to the gun. Try this exercise on a transitional line target like a curling chandelle, or even on a long crosser.

Think about it. How many long crossers have you missed over the top? They looked perfect, didn't they? When we understood this visual phenomenon, we began to realize just how many intermediate and advanced shooters were affected by it, and how many targets were missed as a result. This led us to realize that the overwhelming reason for misses in non-beginning shooters is this partial occlusion. Sure, if the amount of the occlusion were the same each and every time, we suppose you could learn to compensate for it. But why bother? Learn the concept we're going to talk about in the next paragraph—how to play a little farther away from the bird or just under the line during the shot, letting the bird come to the lead in the break point and eliminating the visual confusion. You will find, as we have, that the birds' perceived speed will be much slower, and you will have more time than you ever imagined to insert the muzzles and take the shot.

Playing Away

There is a cure for getting jammed by the target, and it doesn't have to be a measured, mechanical correction. We call it "playing away from the bird." As we said, visual confusion occurs when the gun gets in the picture too early and either blocks the target entirely or confuses the visual input to the brain. If you keep the gun close to the target during the entire swing, you risk having your hand or the barrel or your wristwatch obstruct your focus on the target. Usually it's just one eye that gets obstructed, so your off-eye sees the target and makes the picture feel right; hence, it felt right, but it just didn't break. You need solid output from both eyes for optimum focus.

Playing away from the bird means keeping the muzzles far enough in front of and below the target's flight path so that the barrel stays in the periphery and out of your center of focus.

In talking about this before, we've mentioned that this problem is most common on shots where you have to look across the barrel (right-to-left targets if you're right-handed, left-to-right targets if you're a lefty) although it can manifest itself anywhere. Our solution was what we call the "J" move, or holding the gun slightly lower than you normally would and bringing it to your face in a move that resembles an inverted J. This addressed keeping the barrel lower than the flight path, but we haven't talked much about also moving the barrel away from the bird laterally.

What typically happens with intermediate to advanced shooters is they get on a roll, they're really smashing targets, and so they start to get more aggressive with the gun, moving it closer and closer to the trap each time they call pull. Eventually, they get the gun too close to the trap, and when the bird is launched it jams the gun, so the gun creates a visual occlusion to the target. In some instances, the target is completely hidden from view by the gun. In others, the gun is in the way of only the insertion point (the lead). Because the shooter can see the target in this case, everything appears fine. But if vision on any part of the target or insertion point is distorted or interrupted in any way, a miss will occur. So the problem here is: it looked right, but it didn't break! When this occurs, it typically manifests itself as a timing problem.

Now, one miss isn't that big of an issue, especially if you know the solution. But the real snag with this comes with how most shooters react. They don't know the solution is to simply back off on attack mode a bit and give the target more room. Instead, because it looked right but did not break, they listen to the doubt voice, lose their trust in the subconscious, and try to overcompensate by going mechanical.

When a partial occlusion occurs, there are many different mechanical glitches that can happen. For example, looking at the gun, checking the lead, rushing the mount, sudden erratic muzzle movements, pulling the head off the stock or flinching, just to name a few. These glitches are a direct result of the partial occlusion we're talking about. So if the shooter recognizes the occlusion and eliminates it on the next shot, these glitches will go away. If the shooter doesn't recognize the occlusion, he'll try to fix whatever symptom happened as a result of the occlusion. And we all know what happens when you treat a symptom instead of the disease.

Any time there is an interruption or distortion of visual input to the brain, a miss will occur. In shotguning it manifests itself as a timing problem. This partial occlusion results from playing too close to the bird with the muzzles, or by letting the target jam the gun. You can treat the disease over the symptoms by moving the hold point out toward the breakpoint and keeping the muzzles farther in front of the bird until they merge together in the breakpoint. This will eliminate the occlusion and restore smoothness and consistency to your game. It will improve your ability to focus on the target and maintain that focus through the shot. And you will never experience that bad feeling when it felt and looked right, but did not break.

And when we tell you to play farther ahead of the bird, that doesn't have to be a conscious, measured thing. Usually just by being aware that you've crept closer to the bird, your subconscious can make the fix on the next shot, although it won't make the fix if you let one miss crater your confidence. Stay in feel mode. When you visualize yourself breaking the target, visualize the bird slowly coming to the gun in the breakpoint. If everything about the move felt perfect, it probably was, but it doesn't matter how good the move is if there is a visual occlusion in the immediate periphery ahead of the target, it will look right but will not break! Remember, the gun must be in the breakpoint before the bird arrives to be ahead of it. It's okay to be a little early in the breakpoint.

Peripheral Acceptance

This is a term we use to describe how comfortable a shooter is playing away from the target. For a beginner or intermediate shooter, it seems to be around two to four feet. This means they only feel comfortable with the muzzles pointed at a spot two to four feet in front of the target during the swing. They feel better playing closer to the bird; anything beyond four feet is awkward for them. That's why beginning and intermediate shooters get jammed by the bird more often than advanced shooters, especially on targets that take an excessive amount of lead. On those presentations, it's hard for them to accept the gun way out there without being too aware of it, which pulls their focus off the target and places it on the gun, creating a laundry list of problems.

But the peripheral acceptance for an advanced shooter is much greater, probably between 12 and 30 feet. They've realized that the farther out they play, the easier it is to maintain focus on the front of the target, and the gun never gets in their way. That's how they're able to move so little on all shots, especially the long ones. They let the targets come to them, which requires less movement and makes all presentations seem much slower. That's why they shoot 85 to 95.

Obviously, intermediate shooters will benefit from stretching their peripheral acceptance. That doesn't mean go out and shoot only blazing crossers at 90 mph, or even that you need to shoot long, blazing crossers, what we call Zone Three targets. The majority of your practice should still revolve around targets under moderate speed at a distance less than 30 yards, or Zone One targets, working on building more and more feel.

The practice exercise we suggest for learning how to play farther away from the bird is pretty simple. Take a close target you feel comfortable with, but instead of shooting it with your normal swing, cut the swing in half. If your normal swing on a particular presentation moves your barrel about 24 inches, shoot the target by moving it only 12 inches. To do this, you'll have to start the barrel much closer to the breakpoint and really let the target come to the gun.

This isn't to say that you freeze like a statue while the target is in the air and move at the last minute. Start moving toward the breakpoint as soon as you see the bird, but start the move **much more slowly** than you normally would. It's okay to play with it. See what it feels like to actually miss in front of a target.

The goal of this exercise isn't to hit every target no matter what, because this isn't your normal move. It's a swing that's been shortened in an exaggerated way so you can get used to that feeling. If you continue to make this a regular part of your practice sessions, you should become less anxious about having the gun start well in front while it merges into the lead with the bird at the breakpoint.

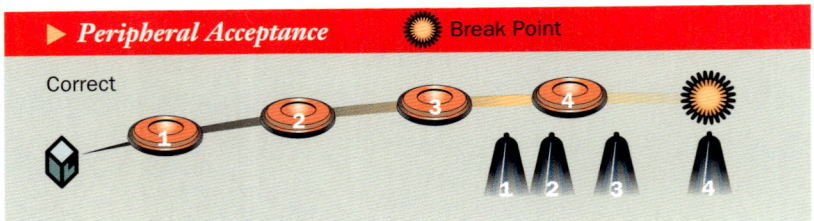

The objective is to start the muzzles much closer to the breakpoint, move the muzzles less and mount the gun much slower—much like a baseball player fielding a fly ball. This takes the gun out of the immediate periphery, eliminating the visual occlusion, and allows the gun to be in the breakpoint before the bird gets there. The gun must be in the breakpoint before the bird arrives in order to break the bird in the breakpoint. It also enables the shooter to easily make any necessary corrections should the bird have an irregular flight path.

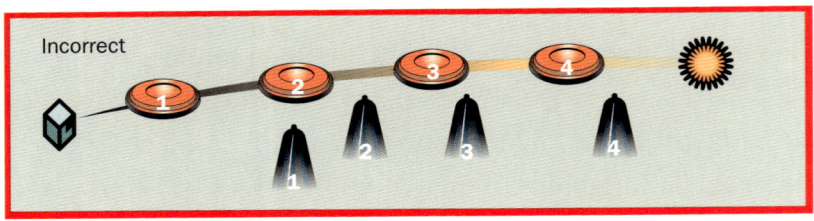

Shooters without an increased peripheral acceptance of the muzzles play too close to the target with the muzzles. The target eventually jams the gun (3), creating the occlusion. When this happens, the shooter can still see the target, but the target is inside the lead that is necessary to break it. Although the gun is in front of the target as the shot is taken, the shooter is actually behind, and the target is missed. It looked right but did not break. This is why shooters have trouble on long crossers or any targets that take excessive amounts of lead. Don't play so close.

Lateral First

There's a key point to remember when practicing the J move and stretching your peripheral acceptance: When the target appears, the first move you make should be lateral. Yes, you will eventually have to get the gun up to your face, but a lot of shooters have the overwhelming tendency to bring the gun vertical to the target line first and then move laterally. When this happens, the bird closes quickly (occlusion), and the shooter ends up chasing, usually in a panic, to catch up. This is not our idea of "merging" the muzzles ahead of the bird at the breakpoint. In traffic, merging at a 90-degree angle is the recipe for a T-bone collision, and in sporting clays, it's the recipe for a miss.

In our method, the breakpoint is the primary target. We play the breakpoint, not the bird. A soft, lateral move at the beginning of the swing is crucial for success. In fact, this wouldn't be a bad swing thought to have, especially if you could come up with a visual to go along with it. See page 35, the one with Steve Brown's swing thoughts. The speed of your gun will get close to matching the target's speed as it approaches the breakpoint, but it's a gradual acceleration. The relative speed of your move will still be determined by the target speed. If the presentation is very slow, your move will be very slow. If the presentation is faster, you can maintain that initial soft lateral move, but your acceleration to target speed will be faster.

Now, because your first move is soft, you must begin to move **as soon** as you see the bird. If you hesitate, it's the same as moving vertically. When you begin to get the input, give the output.

Rare Exceptions

Yes, there are some presentations where a slow, soft, lateral move is not exactly an option—extremely fast targets, window shots, or presentations requiring a breakpoint that's very close to the trap house, for example. On targets like these, you obviously can't make a slow, soft move. You'll have to make pretty quick

Alford Plays Away

One of our students, Brad Alford, is a testament to how well and how quickly the concept of playing away can work. Brad had been struggling because he was missing birds that looked and felt right. His response was to tell himself to "focus harder." Not a bad idea, but for some reason it wasn't working as well as he hoped. When we had a conversation about playing away, however, Brad decided to give it a try at the next tournament.

"I thought about that a lot and said, 'Okay, when that happens to me, I'm still going to say 'focus harder,' but that is not to just look at the leading edge, but to make sure that my move and mount are much better and that I really do have the gun out of the way,'" Brad said. "I will just make sure that I've got the feel of the mount right so that I don't have the gun [too high or too close to the bird]."

At the tournament, playing ahead worked very well for him. "I'd miss one and would just concentrate a little bit more on making sure I got both eyes on the target, and then I could usually run the rest of the station," he said. "I could tell that it helped me to control both how to correct and how to control that confidence. I was not getting the gun up there too close to the line or too close to the trap, making sure that the gun stayed out of the way. It's a very subtle thing; it's easy to do really. So it didn't interfere with any of my routine. It was an easy thing to remember to do that, particularly when something went wrong. I'd go, 'Man, that looked and felt perfect. Well, it must be that the gun got in the way.'"

He was also pretty smart about the way he put the concept to work. He cautioned himself against going mechanical with the move, but when he missed and everything felt right, he would imprint the feel of playing away with the gun before he reloaded. Then he would tell himself to just let go and "feel" the gun ahead of the bird, instead of consciously trying to force it during the shot.

move, although the barrel shouldn't travel more than a few inches, and the direction of its travel will be entirely lateral to the breakpoint. This is where you truly have to rely on your focus and your feel and your commitment to the breakpoint to make it come together. But considering the number of times you'll actually see targets like these—maybe five or ten per 100-bird round—it's a very good idea to practice a soft, lateral first move, playing away from the bird on a regular basis. Make it your normal move, and on the rare occasion that demands a fast move, you'll know to make an exception.

We realize this is conscious mind-oriented, mechanical talk, but it's something you need to practice until it's subconscious. Eventually, you won't have to tell yourself to play away from the bird, it will just be the way you do it. As you get better, you'll be able to start the gun closer to the breakpoint, you'll need less movement to be in sync with the target, and you'll be able to move much more slowly, even on moderately fast birds.

Watch elite shooters and pay attention to how slowly they move and how little actual distance their gun travels. Contrast it with beginning shooters. You'll notice that a telling sign of inexperience is excessive gun speed and excessive gun movement.

Even when the best shooters are on a good score card at the last two or three stations, there is a strong inclination to start the gun just a little bit closer to the trap, even when they don't need to. It's comforting to get that barrel where you can see it really well, but if anything, you should do the opposite.

Chapter Recap

• Before you can connect to a target through feel, you must have a clear view of the target.

- Any time there is distortion or interruption of visual input on the target or insertion point, a miss will occur. A partial occlusion results from playing too close to the bird with the muzzles, or by letting the target jam the gun. The solution is to move the hold point out toward the breakpoint and keep the muzzles farther in front of the bird until they merge together in the breakpoint. Partial occlusion is the culprit when the shooter thinks everything looked and felt perfect, but a miss still occurred.

- Intermediate shooters get jammed by the bird more often because they have a smaller peripheral acceptance than advanced shooters. This means they're only comfortable playing two or three feet in front of the bird, rather than 12 to 30 feet.

- Intermediate shooters can stretch their peripheral acceptance by setting a simple presentation and shooting it with half the movement they would use on a normal target. This forces them to start the gun much closer to the breakpoint and let the target come to them.

> *"...visualization is simply guided imagination; it's taking your inherent ability to fantasize and focusing it."*

Chapter Eight

Visualization

Take a moment to imagine peeling an orange. Picture a big, fat one with a peel that comes off easy and juice that runs over your fingers as you do it. Feel the smooth texture of the outside and the softness on the inside. Smell the strong citrus aroma and listen to the subtle tearing sound as the peel comes off.

If your mind flashed on any sort of mental picture, you just experienced visualization. If the experience was so vivid that you are now salivating, you've got a head start on one of the most powerful tools in shotgunning, or just about any facet of life, in our opinion.

It's pretty amazing when you think about it, that nothing more than a mental image of your own creation—a phantom orange in this case—can produce a concrete physical response. But if that's possible, doesn't it stand to reason that using other mental images on a consistent basis might induce other physical responses, say a smoother, more refined gun mount or the ability to obtain sharper focus on a target? Through our research and first-hand experience, we know this can happen, we've seen it hundreds if not thousands of times, and even if there's only a few things you retain from this book, we urge you to make visualization one of them.

For those new to our instruction, visualization is simply guided imagination; it's taking your inherent ability to fantasize and focusing it. When you hold an unloaded shotgun in your hands, visualize a target and make your move, imagining it exploding into powder, you are stimulating your subconscious and bonding it to your swing. (Remember when we said the subconscious understands pictures, not words?) Sure, your conscious mind might be saying, "What the hell are you doing?" But it deals in rational thought. It wants to control the swing, and it's having a hard time understanding why you're moving to break a target that it can't see. The subconscious sees, however, and it understands perfectly.

Visualization Rules
In *If It Ain't Broke, Fix It!* we advocated a visualization routine of about 15 or 20 minutes a day in a quiet room with your gun, practicing the move on different targets. We still suggest that as a basic visualization routine, but we also urge you to experiment. See how it feels when you visualize with your eyes closed instead of open, with a gun or just with your hands. Try visualizing in different settings; is it easier indoors or outdoors? Does the time of day make any difference? Are you able to incorporate sound, smell, feel, or even taste?

There are only a few "rules" we would give you. The first is to visualize positive results. As strange as it may sound, we've run into people who visualize missing targets, which defeats the purpose. When you visualize, you are programming the subconscious mind through pictures so that it executes the desired result. If you program it to miss, that is what it will execute.

Rule two: Make visualization definitive in plan. Have a specific purpose for the things you visualize and the different types of visualization you do. If you're working to improve specific aspects of your game, you might want to think about what kind of visualization would work best. If you're having difficulty moving your eyes to the second bird of a pair before you move the gun, you should play up that specific part of your visualization routine, really making it crisp.

Rule three: Try to incorporate some type of feel when you visualize. The most ideal way would be to have the actual gun in your hands, moving in concert with the imagined birds, but if you don't have a gun handy, any kind of movement will work. Pretend you have a gun in your hands, or use some kind of substitutes. "Snowflake" Shannon, one of our cohorts, recommends using a wooden dowel or broomstick because it enhances your feel of the slightest movement.

When you are visualizing with the gun, we also suggest that you play the images in your mind as they would appear normally, instead of in slow motion. This goes back to the point on programming your subconscious. With visualization, you are also programming muscular responses. You're telling your brain which muscles to fire and in what sequence to fire them. If you fire them over and over on visualized targets in slow motion, then you're going to embed slow motion responses. One exception here: If your intent is to program a new move, it's okay to do it in slow motion. But if your goal is to practice visualization with your gun, do it in real time.

Different Uses

Our most recent discoveries in the area of visualization have to do with the endless ways you can put it to work. This list is by no means the limit, but here are a few uses we have found:

- *To practice feeling your swing.* This happens almost on its own when you take your (unloaded!) gun and visualize breaking targets with your eyes closed. If you pay attention to how it feels, we think you'll be amazed at all the tiny quirks you pick up that normally escape your attention.
- *During the pre-shot routine.* We've talked about this somewhat in Chapter Six, but we want to stress it again here. When you're picking your breakpoints, visualize the targets exploding in each spot you've chosen. Some people find it very effective to pick the breakpoints and then close their eyes to do the visualization. Others prefer to keep their eyes open and visualize as they're making the plan. Our own visualization does not include a focal point, or where to point the gun before calling pull, because we trust all that work we did in practice to put the gun where it needs to be, away from the bird. If we start thinking hold point, chances are good that we'll go mechanical.
- *To learn a new skill better or faster.* This could be anything from learning to shoot specific targets with a pre-mounted gun (yes, there are some instances when we recommend it) to adding subtle changes to your existing move. In addition to practicing the skill, if you visualize performing it the way you want it, we have to believe it'll be easier to make it a habit. A perfect place to use this would be to help in stretching your peripheral acceptance (page 58).
- *To stay sharp when not shooting regularly or to come back faster after a layoff.* Dean Olson is a prime example of this. He's one of the shooters on our "Coaching Hour," and he once told us that he hadn't touched his target gun in four months during hunting season. He didn't shoot any practice targets on a range, but shot plenty of them in his routine visualization. He went to his first tournament of the

year in Dallas only to have a good time and see where his shooting was, but he ended up shooting extremely well, winning third overall in the main event and second in the five-stand competition.

- *To handle pressure.* In preparing for big tournaments or situations where you know the pressure will be on, visualization is ideal. Visualize the setting and the situation and imagine yourself successfully focusing on nothing but the target, trusting all the training you've done and performing well through it. Include the sights and sounds of a big competition. Those who have done this have found that when they find themselves in the midst of a big competition, a calm comes over them because they realize they've already been there so many times in their visualization.

- *To calm emotion during a shoot.* In this function, visualization can serve like a mantra. A mantra is a phrase used by those who meditate to occupy their minds when other thoughts come in—the goal is to eventually associate a peaceful mindset so strongly with the phrase that it brings the meditative state quickly when uttered. Visualization can be used in the same way. Create a visualization that brings you a centered feeling, use it in practice often, and it will work for you in competition.

- *To fix a recurrent problem.* Let's say that through reading your shooting log, you've discovered a pattern: you aren't keeping your eyes still before you call pull. In addition to tackling this in practice at the range by paying close attention to your eyes, you can use visualization. Visualize shooting targets and keeping those eyes perfectly still before calling pull. If there was a particular tournament when you didn't keep your eyes still, recreate that tournament in your mind, and this time around, visualize yourself doing everything right.

- *To overcome the first station jitters.* Gil used to experience first station jitters and used this method to conquer them. Before the first station at a tournament, he would go out and visualize shooting a ten-target station of five true pairs. He would first visualize shooting it from his own point of view, and then shoot it again from the external perspective of someone watching him shoot. All of the targets were vivid, and he would concentrate on feeling a connection to each one, watching them explode. Then, when he stepped up to the first station, it was no longer the first station, it was the third station for him. Even if you don't get the first station jitters, if you don't have a chance to warm-up on some targets before a tournament, this is a great way to do it.
- *To create a performance script.* Some students, like Steve Mancinelli, have gone so far as to visualize the entire tournament experience, from stepping off the plane to shooting 100 straight in skeet, walking up to the podium, and getting the trophy.

Different Styles

Another beautiful thing about visualization is how personal and varied it can be. When we first began talking and writing about it, we found that a lot of folks made it into "work." That's fine, if it's effective for them to think of it as work, but it certainly doesn't have to be performed this way. As an example, we'd like to share a little story about one of our students, Dick Baker, getting introduced to a different style of visualization by Craig Hill, one of the more experienced shooters we coach.

Dick had a lesson immediately following Craig's session, and we asked Craig to talk with him a little about visualization.

"I expected Craig to turn to me and say, 'Well, Dick, it's sure something you need to work on, it's very essential,'" Dick said.

"But he turned to me, and he started smiling and said, 'It's the best fun you can have.' And he started shooting targets with his hands, just like he was mounting a gun."

For about ten minutes, Craig ran around like a kid with a new toy, breaking imaginary targets. He started inside the tent and then moved outside into the rain. He talked about how he drives down the road, pretending to shoot red lights. He said if he sees a bird as he's walking through the parking lot, he makes his move on it.

"This guy was so into it, enjoying it so much, that it really left an impression with me," Dick said. "It was just like, you've seen boxers warm up in the corner, and you know jabbers just sit there and start moving their hands and warming up."

It was like we'd lit the fuse on a Roman candle, Craig's enthusiasm was that apparent. Craig said, "Man, I just do it everywhere, doesn't matter where it is, I'm doing that. I'll even be sitting there watching TV with my wife, and she will turn to me and say, 'Craig, what are you thinking about?' I'll say, 'Honey, I was just watching some targets break.'"

We think it impressed Dick how every time Craig visualized, his hands were moving like he had a gun in them, and that he was enjoying it so much. "I've been trying to make work out of this," Dick said. "This guy, it was just a fun thing with him. It was fun, but he's getting a lot out of it. He's been doing it so much, and he just enjoys doing it, and that was what impressed me. Quit getting so serious about it. Just go to doing it. Visualize."

We wanted to stress how much positive emotion Craig puts into visualization. If it suits you to do your visualization in a special place like you're praying to the Mother Mary, go for it, but put some positive emotion into it. In our opinion, Craig's method of visualizing all the time, making everything into a target, is a great way to go. We also like that it's childlike, which has a strong subconscious tie.

If you want to watch the masters of visualization, take a look at your kids or grandkids. Children are constantly pretending, and those imagined worlds they create are vivid places that engage all five senses. Two kids playing in the sandbox with toy bulldozers, man, they will be down there on their knees, going "vrooooom vrooooom," really putting a lot of emotion and feel into it.

More Convincing?

If you're not yet motivated to use visualization, we're not sure anything can help you, but here are a few examples that might light a fire under you.

In 1992, a 24-year-old Chinese woman named Shan Zhang won an Olympic Gold Medal in International Skeet, competing against men and women. She posted a world record 200/200 and was the first, last, and only woman to win an Olympic Gold Medal in an open Olympic shooting event. When interviewed about the amazing performance, Zhang attributed much of her success to the fact that she had been visualizing the event from beginning to end, including shooting a perfect score, hearing the crowd cheer and receiving the gold medal on the podium as her national anthem played.

Golf great Jack Nicklaus used visualization all the time; he called it going to the movies in his head. He would visualize where he wanted the ball to finish on a specific part of the green and watch a "movie" of its flight path. He would see its trajectory and behavior on landing. Nicklaus has said that this was the critical element to his success throughout his career, as well as on individual shots and tournaments.

How about some quotes from shooters who use this?

"When I get tired I have a very sloppy mount, which is too much right hand. The only reason I know that is my shooting buddies will tell me, 'Jeez, that looked terrible. Your right hand's there, and the muzzle's bobbing up and down.' I sort of look around rather stunned, totally unaware of it. But since we've been talking about visualizing and I've been working with my eyes closed with the gun in my hand, boy, I picked it up immediately, and it was something I could never do in the field." —**Don Yost**

"I get lazy once in a while with my eyes, and that's one thing I really work on now. Visualizing my eyes going to the second target and seeing it very clearly and then just sticking it. It's just incredible how well it works." —**John Martin**

"I'm shooting differently than I've ever shot before. I finally feel like I understand what you're talking about when you talk about feel. I'll see a pair out on the course. I'll close my eyes and make a move to the break zone, and then look with my eyes and make a move to the next break zone. And when I started doing that, I noticed I was doing all kinds of extra little things." —**Willy Cherry**

"I think that as visualization becomes a more and more common occurrence in your everyday life, that small things trigger it. It can be a car driving by. All of a sudden, the car turns into a target. The headlight. A bird flying through the sky becomes a target and you can fall into that sensation of being in a tournament very easily. You can lose yourself in it. And I think that is really important. You know that you're reaping the benefits of visualization when that starts occurring every day." —**Nathan Pakish**

Free and Feely

So we're beating the point into pulp, but we can't stress enough the power behind this tool. Even though visualization costs athletes nothing but time, we've found that it's a lot like the shooting log—most people don't dedicate nearly as much time to it as they do dinking around on a clays course or buying gadgets to aid in performance.

Pound for pound, visualization is just as valuable as quality practice on the clays range, especially considering what you get out of it for how little you put in. You're spending no money on travel, range fees, shells, or clays, and you're receiving the benefit of enhanced feel. You could shoot a thousand slapdash targets on the range and not enhance feel one drop. Give visualization a month of committed practice, and you will understand what we're saying. You might even consider recording your visualization efforts in your log.

There are so many things that have to come together for you

to have a peak performance. Some you can control and some you can't, and what's important is concerning yourself only with the ones you can control. As you visualize your performance more and more, you'll find the things you can't control will have much less impact on you. Your competitions will become much more subconscious, and your stellar performances will come easier.

One last thing to remember about visualizing: It's okay to smile.

Chapter Recap

- Visualization is one of the easiest and most powerful tools you can use to improve your shooting and your life.

- Visualization is nothing more than guiding your ability to imagine in a consistent way. It is programming your subconscious mind through mental pictures.

- There are only a few rules we suggest for visualization: Only visualize hits, not misses; have a specific purpose for the things you visualize; incorporate some kind of feel when possible, such as visualizing with the gun in your hands; and play mental images in real time instead of slow motion.

- Allow yourself to play when it comes to visualization. It is a powerful tool, but that doesn't mean you have to suck all the fun out of it.

- Professionals and amateurs alike have had proven success with this tool. Use it.

"The basic building block of thought management is learning to handle failure."

CHAPTER NINE

The NEXT STEP

We like to simplify the learning curve into three major stages, and it's a pattern that seems to hold true for just about any activity that requires a lot of analysis in a short time, like shotgunning, basketball, baseball, or operating all the remotes that go with the damn TV.

The stages are subconscious incompetence, conscious competence and subconscious competence. Beginners are in the subconscious incompetence phase. In shotgunning, they're just going out and shooting. They pay no mind to technique, form, or conscious instructions, and they don't know enough about the game to know where they could go wrong. They are letting their subconscious dominate the shot, but it's a subconscious with no database of movement to draw on. Even so, beginners often have amazing results with this method because the subconscious is such a powerful tool when it comes to organizing movement. This is probably why "beginner's luck" is such a well-known phenomenon. Beginners are just out there having fun, and they'll have their share of hits or misses, but they're never really overwhelmed with targets being hard or easy because there's no expectation. They don't know enough about the game to understand how difficult it is!

Eventually, all those who fall in love with the game want to learn how to get better, so they begin to acquire conscious instructions. These can come from a coach, a book, a friend, or whatever, but beginners in any sport will eventually have a laundry list of instructions to give themselves, like, *Stay three feet in front of the bird; keep your left arm straight; keep your eyes still; focus on the back of the rim; choke up when you've got two strikes.* That's how beginners become intermediates. They practice the instructions over and over and enter into the conscious competence phase. They're now competent shooters, but they've almost completely abandoned subconscious performance.

It's at this point that we say a shooter knows enough to be very dangerous to himself. He tends to listen to just about anybody, especially someone who might be able to break a target better than he can. He is constantly thinking about swing mechanics and spends 90 percent of his time practicing mechanics. Although he often emphasizes all the things that are wrong with his game instead of the positive, he still tends to practice all the things that he does well instead of his weak points. This is where the majority of shooters and athletes find themselves, and they probably aren't doing most of the things we've already talked about that will help them advance to the next category on the wings of feel. These are things like keeping a shooting log, occupying the voice, and visualizing. These—and one other weapon we'll talk about—are the gateways to the next level.

Subconscious Competence

Welcome to Nirvana. The place where the sun is always shining, the clays are big as trash can lids, the voice never calls you an uncoordinated asshole, and every stand comes equipped with a cold keg of beer.

All right, not exactly, but the stage of subconscious competence is where elite athletes spend almost all of their time. It is where a shooter has the mind of a beginner but the move and mount of a veteran. At this level, the athlete has done away with nearly all conscious instruction unless they're practicing a specific fundamental or learning a new technique. They know they've put countless hours of practice into breaking targets, so they trust the swing that they've ingrained. Unlike those in the conscious competence phase, they don't try to tackle the whole game, but they spend most of their time mastering the component parts of the game. They are still constantly learning, and they are still practicing fundamentals, refining them to higher and higher levels, stripping away all unnecessary movement. Targets are no longer hard or easy for them because they have trained themselves to give all targets equal respect regardless of whether they're close, far, fast or slow.

The Last Doorway

Like we said, there are several doorways that athletes can take to speed their journey to subconscious competence such as keeping a log to understand their patterns, learning to occupy the voice, and rehearsing with visualization. The last one we're going to talk about is thought management. This is similar to occupying the voice, but it involves much more than the short period of time before you shoot.

When you get to a certain point, your whole game depends on focus . . . and since your focus depends on your thoughts and emotions, you'll want to start with those if you'd like to improve your ability to focus. That's why we've developed a system of thought management.

The basic building block of thought management is learning to handle failure. In truth, that's the biggest part of what we call the mental game: being able to deal with disappointment, with missing targets, with coming up short on your own measuring stick. Success has its pitfalls, but it just isn't the same. You could probably handle investing a dollar and making a million a little easier than you could handle investing a million and making a dollar.

So what's the trick? How are we going to take that sting away? Well, first off, we're not going to try to convince you that dog doody smells like apple pie. Non-achievement is never as fun as achievement, but you almost always learn more from it, and it always makes for a better story in the long run. *Little red riding hood went on a walk to grandma's house and made it there just fine.* Who would want to read that swill? Now, achievement after non-achievement, that's the good stuff.

As for the "trick" to thought management, it's just as simple as changing some of your most entrenched habits and behaviors, not only on the field but at home, in the office—everywhere. Yes, it's a big challenge, but think of it this way: not only will it help your game, it'll make you a lot more fun to be around.

Self-Talk

Sooner or later, you will act out what you think. Your thoughts will become your words and your words will become your actions. Then isn't it completely ridiculous to expect to shoot well if you have a habit of saying things like this after a miss: *That's pathetic. Man, I suck at these! What a terrible shot. This target is impossible. You sonuvabitch, stop moving your eyes before you call pull!*

The thing is, you'll hear this type of talk from a bunch of shooters and a lot of athletes in general. Like we said in Chapter Five, go to any clays range or golf course or basketball court, and we guarantee that these types of phrases—if not much worse—will be the norm. They seem silly when you see them in print, but at one point or another, we've all said them without thinking. We know this because we were just as guilty of it until we made a conscious and consistent effort to change.

Most people say everything but the right thing to themselves when they're in the stand. Talk about pouring on the ridicule. They'll call themselves names that would be fighting words if they came from anyone else. And the things that come out their mouths aren't half as bad as the thoughts that stay in. They give much more emotion to what they do wrong instead of what they need to do to make a correction. Again, we're speaking from experience here.

Self-talk is a big component of thought management. It's about making the voice *your* voice, ensuring that your thought patterns are your own intended creation instead of unthinking fear and doubt-based reactions. The goal is to make your unthinking reactions positive and goal-oriented.

Here are a few examples of self-talk techniques we use with students when they miss and start hollering like a kid who spilled his ice cream. We'll ask them to keep from saying anything after a miss except, "I can break that target if…" No huffing and puffing, no throwing shells, nothing but that phrase: "I can break that target if …" followed by whatever correction they would like to make.

Let's say the shooter didn't have his eyes still before he called pull. All he gets to say is, "I can break that target if I keep my eyes still before calling pull." Then, before he shoots again, he'll visualize keeping his eyes still and smashing the target. This is something we recommend for everyone on every miss: always replay it in your mind as a hit. It's okay to repeat the command "eyes still" before starting the routine, but the routine should be the same once it's started.

We've had great results with that phrase when shooters are open to using it and make an effort to practice. Having a self-talk phrase allows the shooter to move the emotion from what he did to what he intends to do. He doesn't have to pretend the miss didn't happen, but he should accept it, analyze it, and then focus on the present instead of the past. Be consumed with the shot at hand.

Another suggestion we'll give to students who struggle with negative self-talk is to make all of your verbalizations in the stand solution-oriented and with the fewest words possible. Think the problem, emote the solution. Committing to using the fewest words possible forces you to silently analyze the problem and come up with the correct command to give the subconscious in order to produce the desired change. It prevents the whirlwind of negative, judgmental thoughts that the voice produces.

Neutral or Happy

There is virtually an unlimited number of helpful self-talk phrases athletes can use, and we encourage you to come up with your own, those that are uniquely suited to your personality and individual strengths and weaknesses. Experiment to see what types of thoughts increase your concentration, calm you down, or make you feel more confident. Do you have a tendency to rush? Do you grip the gun tightly without realizing it? Pick up on those patterns you've discovered through the log, and tailor your phrases to the things you'd like to work on. Here's a list of good phrases we've come across, just to get you started:

~ The move begins with feel.
~ Commitment to the breakpoint makes it happen for me.
~ I love to shoot a shotgun.
~ Breathe deeply.
~ It's like me to break this target.
~ Laser focus.
~ Just dance with the bird.
~ I am so grateful to be out here.
~ Soft hands, hard focus.
~ Turn it over to the subconscious.
~ It's okay to be early in the breakpoint.

If these don't do it for you, come up with your own. There are only a few boundaries that we've found to be helpful. First, the best self-talk reflects an emotional state that is either neutral or happy. This is the mindset that we strive to have at all times: be either neutral or happy about the result. If you're unable to give positive emotion to something, then give it no emotion at all. A problem is not a problem unless you attach negative emotion to it. Our emotions tend to feed on themselves—they snowball—and it's your choice to make a positive snowball or a negative snowball. Also, what you're doing when you give emotion to something is ensuring that it will happen again. Your emotions are the gatekeepers to the learning process and the performance process. We remember things best when they're surrounded by emotion, whether it's positive or negative. So if you give great negative emotion to your misses, you're really imprinting them in your memory. If you can authentically give great positive emotion to your successes, you're doing the same for every broken target.

What do we mean by "authentically?" That brings us to our second guideline for self-talk: you have to believe it. If you

Gil's Got It

Some of the best rounds I've ever shot, though not score-wise, were those when I had missed too many birds in the beginning and then made a determination, "alright, I'm going to see what it takes to turn this around. I'm going to see what it takes for Gil Ash to turn a poor performance into a good performance. Right now, I'm starting over. I'm going to focus on the birds. I'm going to let it happen, and I'm going to shoot the breakpoints." Because sooner or later you're going to be in a competition where you have a bad stand. And if you've never reached down and pulled yourself up by your bootstraps, that stand is going to perpetuate itself.

You're all going to have performances that aren't your best. That's okay. Remember: you're never out of it until after the last shot, and any time there's doubt, when you begin to evaluate your performance before it's finished, that excites mechanical thinking and makes you rush.

actually hate shooting a shotgun, but you're just doing it because your spouse wants you to, then using "I love to shoot a shotgun" as your self-talk phrase isn't going to help. In truth, nothing will help if you hate shooting a shotgun, but you get the point. If you're not a super positive person by nature, you may want to work on changing that, but in the meantime, try the neutral route.

In addition to the key words of genuine, neutral, or happy, we'll also include *brief* and *objective*. In the stand, self-talk is more effective when it's spoken in a matter-of-fact monotone with very few words, phrases between two and seven words, with no judgmental commentary. A non-judgmental and objective point of view as if you're outside your body looking in seems to work very well. A cool, unemotional analysis will make the cause of a miss clearer and keep you from beating yourself up. Accept a miss for what it was, but avoid evaluating your performance in the sense of good or bad. Just analyze the components of focus, tempo, feel, and trust. When that's through, turn your full attention to the shot at hand.

And Doggone It, People Like Me
Our buddy Stevie Ray brought up a good point on the July 2004 "Coaching Hour." He talked about what he calls "positive sound-alikes." Sometimes what we say is not really what our subconscious perceives, so we think we're telling it one thing, but it's hearing another. An example would be the word "don't," like we talked about before. The subconscious can't understand the word "don't." The positive sound-alikes run along the same lines.

There was a recurring character called Stuart Smalley on the TV show *Saturday Night Live* a few years back, and at the beginning of the skit, Stuart would sit in front of a mirror and tell himself, "I'm good enough, I'm smart enough, and doggone it, people like me." Now it was obvious that Stuart didn't believe any of those things, and that's what made the routine funny. It's also a classic example of the positive sound-alikes. You'll see them in a lot of self-help books. Force-feeding phrases to yourself, even positive ones, isn't going to help if you don't believe them or if you have no evidence for them. That's why we talked about self-talk being authentic.

I can do this; I'm good at this. Yes, these are positive phrases, but saying them before you've ever taken a shot is a form of fear. Just the fact that you feel like you have to say them means you probably don't believe they're true. After you crush a pair of targets and feel that surge inside, that's when it's a good time to enjoy it, congratulate yourself, and feed that positive emotion. *Yeah, man, I smoked 'em. I love shooting these things. I'm getting good at this*. That's authentic. You're in the moment and you believe what you're saying. You're happy, and it's fine to let that out. You haven't forgotten neutral or happy, have you?

Here's a couple more of Steve Brown's positive sound-alikes that might be a surprise: *I'm not going to look at the barrel; I'm not going to think about my score*. This one's a doozy, too: *When I get to the last pair, I'm not going to think about it*. The motivation behind these phrases is great: you'll be more shooty-feely if you focus on the target and not the barrel, or if you dwell on focus instead of thoughts about score or what stand you're on. But if you tell yourself you're not going to look at the barrel, what are you going to do—shut your eyes? The barrel will register in your field of vision. Give your subconscious more specific, visually-oriented instructions. *Laser focus. Cruise missile tracking.* Something like that.

The same goes for thoughts of score or being on the last pair. We're going to talk more about how dwelling on score is not effective thought management, but it's also pretty goofy to expect that you won't think at all about how many targets you're breaking in competition, or that you're on the last stand. If you're shooting well at a tournament, you're going to know it. If you haven't missed any, you're going to know it. So commands not to think about these things are only openings for confusion. One effective technique is to tell yourself that it's okay to let these thoughts pass through. Allow them to happen if they happen, and then move on. This is where the pre-shot routine really starts to work. It's that light switch we've talked about.

Is It Like You?

In our opinion, the most important aspect of thought management is the one that is given the least attention: It is most effective when practiced so regularly that it becomes a habit. In fact, we have heard of very few people who even recommend practicing it. We all go on and on about practicing mechanics, and we spend most of our time doing just that, completely neglecting the mental side of the game. Yes, a solid fundamental move is necessary before a strong mental game is effective, but if you've read this far, then you probably agree that the mental game is the secret to greater consistency. So then why, if you have achieved a consistent move and sound mechanical skills, why would you neglect practicing the mental game, which you've already agreed is the key to the next level?

It must be like you to use effective self-talk phrases, and the best way to accomplish that is by using them everywhere, at all times. Not only on the practice field, but in your car, at your job, and in your personal life. It's self-defeating to let the voice consume you with doubt, fear and anger in your life off the field and then expect to become the master of positivity on a clays range. In fact, whether you realize it or not, you've already got several self-talk phrases that you use when you miss. For the vast majority of amateur athletes, they end in "IT" and are anything but positive. If you can't authentically be positive at first, just be neutral; you shouldn't have to fake being neutral.

To change those habits, we suggest writing down your favorite self-talk phrases in your log, and then making a committed effort to use them so frequently that they become second nature. A committed and constant effort to the "neutral or happy" principle is also a good idea. Begin to focus on thinking only about what you intend to do, instead of what you don't want to happen. The point of practicing it like this is no different than the goal we set for the move and mount: make it subconscious. When positive self-talk comes out of you without any conscious thought, you're on your way to the next level of performance. You won't have to think, "Oh God, that's a doubt thought I just had, now I've got to be positive." It's got to be like you to be positive. But the only way to achieve that is through practice.

Some of the best times to practice the mental game are during idle times, when your body is occupied but your mind is free to wander, just as it is on a clays course. Like when you're driving or cooking or jogging or walking or sitting around the house. Try turning off the TV once in a while and just think about all the good things you've experienced in this game, how many good people you've met, how many good performances you've had, how many good shots you've made. You can do this anywhere, and it's a great activity when you're waiting for someone or standing in line or sitting in traffic. It will probably be a challenge at first, because most people dwell on their failures more than their successes. But sooner or later you will act out what you think, and the things that you give the greatest emotion to, that occupy your mind for the longest period of time, will begin to manifest themselves. The instant your conscious mind thinks it, your subconscious mind works 100 percent of the available time to make it happen. Thought management is nothing more than using that principle to your advantage.

> **A Great Compliment**
> *We were shooting at the U.S. Open a while back and were on a squad with a young man whose parents were watching. At the end of the second day, his mother came up to us and gave us one of the best compliments we've received. She said, "You guys handle missing really well. I've watched you for two days, and when you miss one, it's like it never happened. You just move on." We appreciated that comment more than any, "Wow, you're a great shot" we've ever received because it's such a big part of the mental game, and we work on it constantly.*

Chapter Recap

- There are three stages of learning: subconscious incompetence (beginners), conscious competence (intermediates) and subconscious competence (advanced).

- Intermediate shooters can move to the next level by learning how to get out of their mind (shooting with greater feel). Thought management is the key to doing this on a consistent basis.

- The basic building block of our system of thought management is learning to handle failure. Doing this requires changing some entrenched habits and behaviors.

- Self-talk is one of those. Most people say everything but the right thing to themselves in the stand.

- All of your self-talk should be solution-oriented and in the present. For example, I can break the target if ...

- Come up with your own self-talk phrases and begin to use them until you say them without thinking.

- Strive to cultivate a mindset and self-talk that is either neutral or happy.

- Avoid positive sound-alikes, phrases for which you have no evidence or don't believe.

- Practice thought management in every aspect of your life for the best results.

> **Happily Put My Foot...**
> *Jack Parker is a student who has joined us on the "Coaching Hour" and took the neutral or happy concept in an interesting way. He told us of heading through some heavy traffic while driving to a tournament.* "I was thinking about the last 'Coaching Hour' and you kept saying you have to be happy or neutral," *Jack said.* "I'm not used to driving in the city, and the first few people that cut me off, I was kind of mad and unhappy. But I said, 'no, I can be neutral or happy, and if they'd pull over I'd happily stick my foot in their butt.'"
> Well, at least humor is better than anger. Keep working on that Jack.

"...emotional control is what self-coaching is all about. And ultimately, the best coach for your mental game is going to be you."

CHAPTER TEN

SELF-COACHING *and* THOUGHT MANAGEMENT

More than their sheer physical talent, the greatest athletes in sports history—like Michael Jordan, Wayne Gretzky, Martina Navratilova, Tiger Woods, or Mia Hamm—possess both uncommon emotional control and unlimited passion for what they do. By staying so strong in their habits, routines, and practice to keep emotions in check, they become constants in a world of inconsistencies. Their achievements are not a result of feeding negative emotions, but from coming out of failure with no loss of enthusiasm.

This emotional control is what self-coaching is all about. And ultimately, the best coach for your mental game is going to be you. Coaching yourself mentally and emotionally is a huge part of consistency and success. That's why our intention is to help our students acquire the tools they need to become outstanding self-coaches.

Emotion controls the learning curve in the development of a strong mental game, and in addition to self-talk, there are a few other tools and exercises we advocate in the quest to guide your own emotion. But first, to understand exactly how emotion works in competition, we'd like to examine two general patterns that most performances follow. It comes from a two-part article written by Lynn Mariott and Pia Nilsson in *Golf For Women* magazine. It was a unique piece that broke down performances in two ways, the upward or downward spiral. The upward spiral is the one that leads to zone experiences, while the downward spiral leads to a crash in performance.

The Downward Spiral

First, we should note that **both** spirals begin at a neutral state. There's no emotion involved at this point. You aren't too excited or too fearful. For some shooters, the neutral state is still intact on the first stand, although it's definitely possible to have positive or negative emotion before you ever fire a shot. Now, the downward spiral goes from the neutral emotional state to one of **hesitation**. This happens when you first experience adversity or failure and you can't control your emotions on targets you miss. You become hesitant. The voice of doubt is there. You check the lead. Mechanical thought begins to creep in, and you second-guess your swing or hold point or foot position or breakpoint.

The next phase is **confusion**. Because you're no longer relying on focus, feel, or trust, nothing is working. You're consumed with mechanical questions. Was I ahead? Was I behind? Was the plan wrong? You'll try anything, from changing your mechanics to asking your squad mates, "What am I doing wrong?" Our friend Dean Olson describes this as "going crazy." Your feel is gone.

The progression then moves to *frustration*. The voice is no longer in your head but is coming out of your mouth in the form of negative self-talk. I'm shooting like crap. What is wrong with me? God, I always do this. Oh great, another fast crosser, I didn't touch the last one.

From frustration, it's a short leap to *anger*. Once the performance has hit this stage, it's extremely difficult to get back. Blame and judgment, the children of doubt, come on strong. These targets are bullshit. Whoever organized this tournament is an idiot. I shouldn't have come. You're pissed off, and you just want it to be over.

Depression is the last stop on this manure train. Your self-worth is now totally attached to the performance. Through this experience that lasted only a few hours in a game that is supposed to be a fun pastime, you've come to see yourself as a complete failure in life. *Why do I even do this? Why do I spend money just to have my name posted on a scoreboard to be humiliated?*

The Upward Spiral

Before we analyze the sad downward spiral, let's take a look at its counterpart. Again, you're beginning in a neutral state with no expectation. You're there simply to perform. Your mind is clear, and you have solid training to back you up. After a few shots, maybe a couple of pairs or a whole station, you go from the neutral state to being *interested* in what you're doing. You're in the game now, excited about shooting. Each station is a puzzle, and you're there to solve the puzzle of breakpoints, how to take the pair, and how to allow your strong focus to take over for each shot. Because of the interest you have, you're totally in the present at each station.

From interest, you move to a new level of feeling *engaged*

in the game. There is no longer a casual interest in playing it; you are completely committed and consumed. The plans become more obvious, as do the breakpoints. You have no fear about breaking the targets because the voice of doubt is totally tied up in your commitment to the breakpoint. As a result, you are beginning to feel more connected with each target. Regardless of the outcome of your shots, you become more centered with each one.

Out of this feeling, you become **confident**. Your belief in each plan grows, as does the trust in your ability to execute the plan. You have the feeling that no matter what kind of targets they throw, you can deal with them. If a miss occurs, it's analyzed, dealt with in a non-judgmental way, and corrected. It's as if you don't really even notice the misses, just the solutions.

Somewhere after the confidence stage is the **zone**. You have continued to feed on focus, feel and trust to the point where everything just flows. There are no mechanical thoughts about technique or lead; it's simply breakpoint one, breakpoint two, breakpoint one, routine, and pull. Focus and feel come with ease. Your body and mind are working together without effort, and you feel like you're just there taking part.

Maybe a few more stations pass and you seem to transcend into a **euphoric state**. You're happy. It's easy. There's no gun, just targets and breakpoints. Your internal pharmacy is manufacturing healthy chemicals that maintain this state of relaxed concentration. Everything seems to happen without your influence. Your buddies have to tell you when it's over. You have been so deeply involved in feel and focus that you don't realize you've finished the last station.

The Progression
For us, the most noteworthy aspect of the spirals was how one

step led to another. In the upward spiral, it was ***neutral*** to ***interested*** to ***engaged*** to ***confident*** to being in ***the zone*** to ***euphoric***. In the downward, it was ***neutral*** to ***hesitant*** to ***confused*** to ***frustrated*** to ***angry*** to ***depressed***. It's important to understand that you don't go straight from neutral to depressed or from neutral to euphoric. The zone is a product of how well you assemble the right ingredients for peak performance and handle the emotional transition from station one through the middle of the course and all the way to the end. Notice that we didn't say anything about how you shot from station one into the middle of the course. The same goes for the downward spiral. The angry and depressed state is a result of feeding your negative emotion.

This is important to understand, as many people seem to believe that positive emotion is a product of shooting well and negative emotion is a product of shooting poorly. In our experience, the opposite is true. You shoot well because you associate with positive emotion; you feed the upward spiral. You shoot poorly because you associate with negative emotion and feed the downward spiral.

Something else to ponder about these categories of performance: Isn't it reasonable to assume that if you have a habit of negative thought, you'll handicap yourself, and if you have a habit of positive thought, you'll be giving yourself an advantage? If you walk around in a perpetual state of hesitation, confusion, frustration, anger or depression, how can you expect to jump right into an upward spiral? And it works the other way, too. If your natural state is usually one of interest or engagement in the world around you, wouldn't it be easier to build a zone experience? Hmm, maybe there is something to practicing this self-talk.

We've been around this sport long enough to experience

both these spirals and witness others going through them, and it's clear to us that the shooter's reaction emotionally to whatever happens when he shoots determines which spiral he's going to take. We'd also like to reiterate that each spiral begins with neutral. You can't force yourself to be happy about a miss, but you can allow yourself to stay at neutral. From there, you can still enter the upward spiral, but if you don't stop and discard the emotions that create the downward spiral by the phase of hesitation or confusion, it's almost impossible to turn it around. So if you recognize signs of the downward spiral in your performance, teach yourself to return to a neutral state. How do you do this? Glad you asked.

Disassociation and Non-judgmental Thought
When you give emotion to an experience, it becomes part of you. It hangs around. But when you miss, you can learn to return to a neutral state by practicing disassociation. And on the flipside, you can practice associating positive emotion with your successes. This is usually a little easier to do, and that's why we stress disassociation. When you miss a target, practice giving it absolutely no emotion. Remain neutral. When you're disassociated with something that has happened, it can't control you and it won't linger. That's not to say you should pretend it didn't happen. Just acknowledge it, accept it, learn from it and move on.

There's a simple exercise we like to use to practice this concept. When you go to practice, set aside some time for disassociation. Shoot three stations, but shoot them with only one purpose: to remain neutral and non-judgmental the entire time. Shoot with no emotion whatsoever. Avoid thoughts like good or bad. Just make the plan, follow your routine, and pull the trigger. Maintain an internal and external poker face, regardless of the result. No messing with mechanics, no frowning, no cussing, no nothing. When you get through shooting the stations, analyze your performance based on how well you were able to stay neutral, not on how many targets you broke. The reason we say "no emotion" instead of "only happy emotion" is so you can get a feel for what it's like to stay in neutral. You don't have to think about trying to force happiness, just stay at zero. If it's difficult for you, try to figure out why it was so hard. This will give you some insight into how much you're really able to control your own emotions and what areas give you the most trouble. This is usually a more challenging exercise than people think—but we said it was simple, not easy.

To more graphically illustrate the point, we tried this type of exercise with a group of students in southern Colorado. We gave everybody 30 golf tees in the morning and told them we'd like to find out just how many negative thoughts they had. We asked them to give us one of the golf tees any time they experienced a negative thought. Every time anyone said something negative, they had to give us one back. If it looked like they were thinking something negative, they had to give us one back. The results were interesting. Just the fact that they were afraid to give the golf tees back made a few start thinking negatively. Some of them had given us all the golf tees before they ever got to shoot the first stand.

Most of us aren't usually aware of how easy it is to associate with negativity and how easy it is to sell to other people. But if you intend to self-coach, it's important to recognize it so you can get better and better at disassociation.

Here's another disassociation exercise to try: Go out and shoot targets, but refrain from making any corrections. Make that the point of the exercise, to simply observe your move and mount, and rate the quality of the session based on how well you were able to resist the temptation to correct yourself. Even if something feels off, resist the urge to change it during that session. Avoid judgments of any kind regarding your swing or breakpoints or mental focus. Simply take note of what's there as objectively as possible. You can try this off the range, too, if you really want a challenge. How do you know when you're succeeding? When you attain such an objective state of mind that you find yourself saying things like, "Oh, that's interesting, that guy just cut me off and flipped me the bird," and saying it as if you were talking about the weather.

OSP Correction Routine
We typically see shooters wanting to hurry up and load the gun and quickly call for another pair when they miss. They don't want to face the fact that they missed or failed. And when they do acknowledge the miss, it's usually accompanied by an excuse or two. It's as if they are running away from the miss. All this does is perpetuate the miss and does nothing to correct the miss on the next shot. The people who win at sporting clays are not the ones who never miss; they are the ones who miss, but correct it on the next shot and run the station out.

The first thing we see when people miss is they look down, hanging their heads in disgust or despair. When we ask them what they're doing, they usually say that they're trying to visualize what happened. Why try? Why not first admit that you missed the target(s) and look up into the breakpoint to visualize what happened? It's easier to visualize what happened by looking in the breakpoint where it happened, rather than trying to visualize while hanging your head in shame. Losers look down. Winners look up.

Here is a correction routine we've developed that has helped many shooters become more consistent, not only with their

corrections, but also with their scores. When a miss occurs:
1. Admit that you missed the target.
2. Stop. **Look up!** Look immediately back into the breakpoint where the miss occurred. Face it.
3. Replay what happened.
4. Analyze it and make a change. Believe the change. Be determined to make the change on the next shot. Visualize the change occurring and the target smoking.
5. Then and only then load the gun. Don't even grab your shells to load until you have taken steps 1 through 4 and you believe the change.
6. Load the gun and start your pre-shot routine. Call pull and break the targets.

With this routine you will be shocked at how obvious the reason for the miss becomes and how obvious the correction is. You'll also be shocked at how easy it is to stay in a positive frame of mind and body. The tendency to give negative judgmental commentary about yourself or your performance will almost instantly go away because you are concentrating on the correction. Suddenly you'll find yourself in the present and in control of your game, mechanically and emotionally.

You'll be surprised at how quickly you want to load the gun and call pull after you miss the first few times you try to implement this routine. It's okay. Laugh at yourself. (You might as well, everyone else is.) When you hurry to load the gun and call pull after a miss without committing to changing something, rarely will the result change. The quickest way to get out of a hole is to *stop digging*. The only experience worthwhile is the successful or unsuccessful attempt of a plan. If the change creates a success, duplicate it. If not, change something else on the next pair. At least you have eliminated one possible cause.

Never miss the same targets the same way two times in a row. Use the correction routine to change something. Make the plan, shoot the plan.

Post-shot Routine

If pre-shot routines and correction routines are good, a post-shot routine is even better, because it means you were successful in executing your plan. The targets are powder. Enjoy that! And we're serious when we tell you this. It's easy to say, "oh, everyone enjoys it when the targets break, I don't have to tell myself to do that," but you'd be surprised how few shooters really do take a moment to reinforce how good it felt. That's important—just as important as the correction routine, which is a form of post-shot routine. That doesn't mean you have to act like some of these NFL players who score a touchdown and take five minutes to do an end zone dance, but we highly recommend that you create a short routine that you use after the targets break.

Again, if you'd like strong visual depictions to go with our advice here, we would direct you to look at our new DVD that covers all the routines we teach. It's called *Sporting Clays Pre-Shot Routine* and is available on our website www.ospschool.com.

In Chapter Nine we talked about using self-talk that is "neutral or happy," and this is a part of that. In fact, the post-shot routine is one place where we'd almost insist on "happy." If you think it works better for you to stay in neutral the entire time, that's your call, but you should at least acknowledge inside of yourself that breaking those targets feels so damn good. Personally, we like to verbalize it, let our happy emotions show.

You know how professional dog handlers recommend that you train your dog on a reward-based system? The dog does something you're proud of, so you reward it, and you do that over and over again until it's a habit. The dog associates the action with the reward and begins to do it automatically. Well, we're not going to start calling any of you Fido, but our bodies and brains all work on that same principle. If we give ourselves positive feedback, really enjoy those things that feel good, like breaking targets, we're conditioning ourselves to do it over and over again.

You understand? Good boy.

Who You Calling Minutia?
Like many shooters, we used to think the most challenging part of any shooting sport was the period of time surrounding the shooting experience, the time just before stepping into the stand and the time spent analyzing and shooting targets. Through experience and study, we've come to see the time between stands as equally important. Similar to golf, the large amount of time spent between shots or stands is one of the unique aspects of our sport. Unlike sports such as tennis, basketball or football, there is a great deal of idle time to think. This makes a strong mental game even more important. So we came up with a system to address the time between stands. Big surprise, huh?

Some of our students have come to call this Gil Ash's Minutia, because minutia is the key to the whole thing. The jist of this method is to find some trivial, non-judgmental, non-shooting-oriented thing to occupy your mind during the idle time. If you're waiting to shoot, once you've made your general plan and prepared your equipment, it's counterproductive to sit around thinking about mechanics or agonizing over whether your plan is right. Trust the game you've brought. Watching every single target of every other shooter on your squad is another big energy waster. When you do this, you're expending your critical time bank of focus that we've mentioned before. If you honestly feel it's necessary to watch the targets of another

> **Gil's Guidance**
>
> *Here's one of my original minutia that I'd use between stands. It played a big role in the Browning-Briley Tournament a while back, and I'd like to outline it for you. My goal for the tournament was to stay completely focused on NOTHING between stands. That was the goal I wrote in my log. At each new stand, I would go up, look at the presentation and make my plan with breakpoints. I'd put my chokes in, make sure I had my shells right, and then I'd put the gun in the Clays Car and walk away.*
>
> *Now, back when I was working through college, I was part of an asphalt crew. There was a guy on the crew named Kenneth Treadway who always wore a cowboy hat and cowboy boots, and he always smoked Viceroy cigarettes. I hadn't heard of Viceroys for years, so I asked him why he smoked them. He said, "Cause Viceroy's a thinking man's cigarette." So now, in between stands, I walk around looking for a Viceroy cigarette butt. That's about as close to nothing as I can think of, and that's my minutia.*
>
> *It's just something to occupy my mind, because the only thing I need to do on game day is make the plan and shoot the plan. If I'm not making the plan or shooting the plan, I'm occupying my mind with something else. And that's especially critical when I'm shooting well and coming down the home stretch, when the brain wants to dwell on the finish line.*

shooter to determine the best plan for you, that's fine, but once that plan is determined, head for the minutia.

There are thousands of different things you could choose to be your minutia, but here are a few examples. Walk around looking at the bugs on the ground. Think about the fishing trip you're going to take next week; run through the list of gear you'll need. Juggle shotgun shells. If you're not self-conscious, sing some songs.

It can be anything you want, but the more the activity absorbs your attention, the better. It's also best if you find something that isn't really going to tax your eyes, so we would stay away from reading or watching birds, which would otherwise be good activities. The point of Gil Ash's Minutia is to help you stay in that neutral mental state, or whatever stage of the upward spiral you might be in. It's like putting your brain on idle. If you're interested, it will help you stay interested. If you're confident, it will help you stay confident. If you're hesitant, confused, or angry, hopefully it will pull you back to neutral. Again, as long as it's unimportant and non-judgmental, go for it.

Chapter Recap

- Self-coaching is ultimately about emotional control.

- The upward and downward spirals in performance are a result of feeding positive or negative emotion.

- Both spirals begin at the neutral state, so remaining in a neutral state after failure is huge. You do this through disassociation and non-judgmental thought.

- Disassociation is about giving absolutely no emotion to a miss. It's about accepting it, learning from it, and moving on.

- An exercise for practicing disassociation is to practice shooting three stations with no emotion whatsoever. Avoid thoughts of good or bad. Analyze the performance based on how well you were able to stay neutral, not by how many targets you broke.

- Develop a correction routine. This is simply a pre-shot routine applied to the event of a miss.

- Eventually *everything* that happens after you pull the trigger is only feedback, nothing more!

- Gil Ash's Minutia is a great way to preserve concentration and focus between stands. It involves occupying your mind during idle time with some trivial, non-shooting-oriented, non-judgmental thing, like finding Viceroy cigarette butts.

- The OSP correction routine is:
1. Admit that you missed the target.
2. Stop. **Look up!** Look immediately back into the breakpoint where the miss occurred.
3. Replay what happened.
4. Analyze it and make a change. Believe the change. Be determined to make the change on the next shot. Visualize the change occurring and the target smoking.
5. Then and only then load the gun. Don't even grab your shells to load until you have taken steps 1 through 4 and you believe the change.
6. Load the gun and start your pre-shot routine. Call pull and break the targets.

"In a game as full of failure as sporting clays, how you react and handle the failure determines the level of your success."

CHAPTER ELEVEN

SCORE PLATEAUS *and* SLUMPS

The view from a plateau is great—you can see the valley you left behind—but it's also flat. You're no longer climbing. Yes, we're talking about those rugged mountain thingies related to mesas and buttes, but it's also true for sports performance. We call it a plateau when your scores level off due to a lack of knowledge, experience, or commitment. You've gone as far as you're going to go based on the current quality of your move and mental game. When you get there, three things can happen: you can pitch your tent and make that flat spot your home, you can keep climbing, or you can stumble down the other side.

Since you have your hands on this book and are still reading, we're throwing out option one. Maybe you forgot to bring a tent to pitch. Option three, stumbling down the other side, is also known as a slump. It's something that happens, but it doesn't have to, and we'll deal with it a little later on. Anyway, the whole point of being here is to keep climbing, right? So let's climb.

Common Plateaus

If you want to keep climbing beyond a plateau, change is inevitable. It's the quality of your move and mental game that has you at the top of the plateau, and you'll continue climbing when you elevate that quality. That's the reason you should always look forward to a plateau, because something great is up ahead. It means you're about to learn or master something new.

Here are the common plateaus we see people reach in sporting clays:

- Starting at 50 percent. Most beginners tend to score in the 50 range. This is the subconscious incompetence phase. They have no approach and no guesses about method. They just load the shell, call pull, and squeeze the trigger.
- Then they get hooked and move to 65 with regular practice and greater experience with the six different trajectories. They've started to think about foot position, hold point, swing mechanics, and lead. The game is a lot of fun for them, and they devour copious amounts of instructional material, which eventually gets them to the next plateau.
- The next level is a fluctuation between 72 and 78. It's where the greatest number of shooters reside in our sport. They have practiced a good deal on the mechanics of their move and have developed a fairly good move and mount, but only one or two swing speeds: fast and faster. Because they have not developed different swing speeds, they are unaware of feel and are stuck in the phase of conscious competence. They almost always listen to the voice and check the lead, and with rare exception, the conscious mind is involved in every shot. We have yet to see someone in the conscious competence phase shoot better than a 78 or 79, unless the targets are very fluffy.
- Breakpoints have been discovered! This brings the next

plateau of 81. The shooter has learned to make a rough plan before stepping into the stand, picking the spots where they intend to shoot the targets. They have refined their move through practice off the field, using things like the flashlight exercise or visualization. They've realized the importance of gun speed staying the same as target speed, and they have adjusted their move accordingly. They're beginning to feel.

- Next stop, 84. They've begun work on pre-shot routine and understand the importance of tying up the voice just before and during the shot. Their move is beginning to mirror the target's speed and line. Feel is increasing. Because their move is more in sync with the bird, it is becoming easier to not only commit to a breakpoint, but to shoot the birds in the breakpoint.

- They go from an 84 to an 86 because they are really starting to feel. This has occurred through improving the move and pre-shot routine, and advanced work with visualization. They are even more aware and committed to the breakpoints, and they are tying up the voice on a fairly regular basis. They are beginning to see certain trajectories that always give them problems and they're determined to dominate them. To go any higher in score, they must change the way they practice. Instead of simply shooting the course, they should practice their weaknesses to turn them into strengths.

- More feel allows them to begin to trust, which is a springboard to 88. Because practice sessions are higher quality, everything is becoming more subconscious. Shooters at an 88 average understand that they must trust the subconscious in order to win.

- Here's the big jump. When shooters fully commit to trust through feel, they go from an 88 average to a 92 or 93. They have fully entered the subconscious competence phase and have learned to tie up the voice on a very consistent basis. The immense feel they have allows them to trust the breakpoint and feel the target broken before they pull the trigger. Their pre-shot, post-shot, and correction routines are flawless and fully subconscious, and they have mastered the ability to stay neutral between stands. They learn from failure and move on. Each practice session, they shoot 100 targets for score to get more comfortable facing the scorecard. They work on stations that give them problems, and they always train on one of the six different trajectories during each practice session.

- Shooters stay in the 90s because of feel and because they know how to practice the right way. The best of the best—those who will often break 97, 98, or 99—are able to do so because they have learned how to create their zone experience and because they are able to create a bubble in the stand where the voice never gets in.

In our instruction, we have seen these plateaus many, many times, and there is rarely an exception. We urge our students to study this break-down frequently because it provides a good roadmap for what you'll need to learn based on your average. If you'd like advice on what to practice for each step of the plateau, you're in luck, because we're going to tackle that issue in the next chapter. For now, our basic recommendation is to seek qualified help at each plateau. An experienced instructor can guide you to the most efficient way to learn and ingrain the skills that will get you climbing again.

How to Make a Slump

If you'd like to stumble off the other side of the plateau, all you have to do is get frustrated that you're flat-lined and give a lot of emotion to failure. That ought to get you into a slump in no time. It's hard to agree with when you're experiencing one, but slumps are self-induced. They are plateaus with a dollop of negative emotion.

Generally defined, there will be a ten to twenty percent decrease in scores during a slump, rather than scores topping out in a two- to six-bird deviation as they will during a plateau. A 90 average will typically drop to the low 80s. A 60 average will tumble to 50. Remember that we're talking average here. It doesn't mean you're in a slump if you have one or two substandard performances.

There's also what we'd call a mini-slump, where a shooter struggles with a certain aspect of the game, rather than the whole thing. An example would be, *I can't buy a rabbit.* Or a teal, or a right-to-left crosser, or low five if you're a skeet shooter—whatever the problem target might be.

> "No improvement happens without change. For every change there is a price. The value is in the commitment."
> —*Vicki Ash*

But a major slump, man, this is usually where people start asking themselves: *Why do I even do this?* It comes from a deep emotional connection between score and self-worth. If you connect those two, this sport is going to wreak havoc on you. As one of our students, John Gibson, puts it, "This sporting clays game is the only game I know of that you can pay good money to go to a shoot, have your name put up on a board, and be publicly humiliated … and do it again next week."

So not only do elite athletes have a high tolerance for failure, they also grade their performances against their commitments and goals. Those who compare their performances against others are destined for mediocrity. You just can't do it in this sport and expect to achieve your fullest potential.

Another reason people tend to struggle with slumps is because they don't have a clear picture of why they play the game. In many cases, their dreams have become their expectations with no commitments to achieve them. This is usually true for shooters who have moved up quickly through the classes. They expect to keep advancing at the same rate without putting any more time or energy into training or practice. And they expect to do it through conscious, mechanical shooting. This is why those who give up the game usually do so when they're averaging 72 to 78. At this point, if you can't turn loose of shooting lead, and you measure yourself against those who do, attaching your self-worth to score, you're in a perfect position for disappointment. Understand that the better you get, the more effort it's going to take to keep moving up, but once you commit to subconscious, feely shooting, you are on your way. Keep in mind that those who wish to do great things often encounter great obstacles. Be patient in your curve!

> "It's not what you know that makes you better. It's what you're willing to learn."
> —*Gil Ash*

Stop Digging

If you're in a slump and are ready to put down the shovel, here are a few ideas for getting out of the hole. For starters, go ahead and shut off the emotion hose. Pumping in fear, frustration, or anger will only deepen the slump. Accept that it's merely a wake-up call. Just like a plateau, a slump is an indication that you are about to elevate your performance to another level. Never fear a slump because you will always come out of it much stronger. It's just your game telling you there's something that needs to be corrected.

Secondly, know that whatever needs to be corrected is nothing major in most instances. Slumps are almost always indicative of very small problems that manifest themselves on different targets on different days. Most often, it's one fundamental that has slipped a little at a time, so you've been able to ignore it for a while. For shooters averaging above the

> **Other Shooters' Advice**
>
> When you ask other shooters for help they will typically try to help you by getting you to hit the target the way they do. As long as they are with you, you can shoot pretty good. But when you are by yourself, your performance will suffer. Even well-intentioned advice from another shooter is rarely a long-term fix.
>
> For instance, let's say you're missing behind a left-to-right crosser. You ask a shooter who can hit the target for help. Chances are they will see that you're missing the target behind and tell you to give it more lead. What they won't do, is try to figure out why you're behind. But you already know you must be ahead of the target to hit it. So the question is not, "Where were you?" The question is, "Why didn't you get to where you already knew you were supposed to be?"
>
> Without even looking at the target you're shooting, an experienced coach can look at your move on a given target and tell you where you missed, and more importantly why. There are many reasons a shooter gets behind a target. The misplacement of the shot cloud is the result of the miss, not the cause. The true cause of a miss is usually lack of focus on the front of the target, poor tempo (moving and mounting the gun too fast or playing too close to the target) or poor gun mount where the gun doesn't get to the face.

mid-70s, that fundamental is traceable to one common root—feel. While there can be many symptoms for loss of feel, excessive muzzle speed is the most prominent. This is especially true for rabbits, quartering birds, and slow crossers. If you find yourself struggling to hit these targets, your game hasn't gone in the toilet; you've simply lost your feel, which causes you to move the gun faster and faster.

It's also good advice to seek help for a slump. Some of our students have expressed concern that asking for help might be like giving in to the problem or attaching negative emotion to it, but we don't agree. Seeking advice is a positive, solution-oriented direction. Don't they always say that acceptance is the first step to recovery?

As we study sports vision more and more, observing some of

the phenomenal things that athletes can do by simply focusing on an object and subconsciously reacting to the visual input, it becomes very apparent to us that shooting a shotgun is more a visual game than a game of swing mechanics and lead. When your eyes, your subconscious brain and your hands are truly connected, the target doesn't have a chance. When a miss occurs, we've found that there was an interruption or distortion in the visual input to the brain. The better the focus, the better the shot. How could you possibly expect to hit the target if you were not focused intently on it? You must eventually learn to train your mechanics to allow you to maintain intense focus on the target, trusting yourself to put the gun where it needs to be.

It's even more important in this situation to take some care in whom you ask. It's almost an automatic response to go to anyone who can hit the birds you can't, but be cautious if they concentrate on **where** you're missing instead of **why**. It's impossible to get to the core of the issue by addressing a symptom.

So if a loss of feel is usually at the core, how do we suggest getting it back? Will it involve a colonic, lots of wheatgrass juice, and strategically placed crystals? No, (and why would you even suggest such things?) the key is actually in cupcakes. That's right, go shoot some cupcakes. That's probably got you visualizing, doesn't it?

For the uninitiated, a cupcake is an easy, straightforward target, something like a slow, left-to-right crosser at 20 yards. The least effective thing you could do is force yourself to practice whatever targets you're having trouble with. Get away from those, back off on the difficulty, and concentrate on shooting targets that are comfortable. And here's another big key: When you shoot the cupcakes, concentrate on feel. If you can't get the feel back right away, keep shooting them until you do.

Typically, shooters want to go conscious with their correction if they find themselves in a slump, and this only makes a deeper hole. It's a natural reaction; we all learned the mechanics of the game consciously first, so that is immediately where the domineering conscious mind wants to go. But instead of letting the voice boss you around, try relaxing into the slump. Look for feel, that connection to the target. It's not necessary to try to fix every single thing you think might be the problem. Just shoot some cupcakes, pay attention to the way your swing feels, and don't try to change anything at first. Use your routine and really commit to the breakpoints. When your feel gets stronger, the small fundamental that has slipped will probably become very apparent.

Short of a lesson, the relaxed, back-to-basics approach is the best thing we can advise. It doesn't matter the level; whether you're a 55 or a 95 percent shooter, we all have to go back and revisit basics. Learn to recognize and accept a dip in your average, but there's no reason to attach anxiety and emotion to it. Go subconscious and look to regain feel and trust. Know that you're about to elevate your performance to the next level.

Is It Mental or Mechanical?

Although it's impossible to completely separate the mental game from the mechanical game, we're including this section because so many shooters come to us claiming to have either a mental or mechanical problem. Sometimes, a shooter who thinks he has a mechanical problem is really suffering the most from a poor attitude or being eaten up by the voice, or a shooter thinks she's got a mental problem and is actually most in need of some simple practice on the fundamental move and mount. Of course, a shooter can always have mental *and* mechanical problems; a mechanical problem can become a mental problem and vice versa.

Danny Finds Feel

Student Danny Cummings had an experience that testifies to the power of going back to basics. Danny was averaging in the mid- to upper-70 range and feeling good about his game when everything seemed to fall apart.

"I went to a tournament with about 120 guys there. It was about 95 or 100 degrees, and we're shooting," he said. "But there was no feeling at all the whole day. I was getting in the stand, I was looking at the bird, but it was like someone put a sack over my face every time I pulled the trigger."

Danny said his brother called a few days later and pointed out that Danny wasn't shooting at all like he'd been shooting the last few months.

"My brother said, 'Usually you get up there and right as the gun gets to your face, you pull the trigger and you break the bird,'" Danny said. "I thought, well, maybe I'll call Gil and Vicki. No, I won't do that. Maybe I'll go get a lesson. No, I won't do that. All I did was listen to the ['Coaching Hour' CD] on slumps."

As he was listening to the "Coaching Hour," the light came on. "I was listening to it and was like 'Jesus Criminy! They're describing me right here,'" he said. "On the tape, Gil describes the slump and what to do, so I went back to basics."

Danny got the flashlight out, put it in the gun and started practicing his mount. After that, he went out to the field, loaded the trap and started moving the gun to the breakpoint ahead of the bird, looking for feel.

"Just in a matter of a week from that tournament, it was all coming back," Danny said. "Just move your eyes and that gun ahead of the bird. It's like Gil told me, 'You've got two choices when shooting a target. It's either here it comes *or* there it goes.' And I like here it comes."

We do too, Danny, we do too.

In general, however, we find that the root of a shooter's problems is usually mentally or mechanically based. If it's mechanical, the back-to-basics approach is a perfect prescription. If it's mental, that approach is still good, but the negative self-talk or lack of routine or inability to tie up the voice must be addressed before big strides can be made.

To help with the diagnosis, we've included four questions that can point you in a solid direction:

- **Are you satisfied with the skill level you have when you're shooting well?**
  This is important to ask because no amount of mental rehearsal or voice control will help if you don't have good technical and mechanical skills. Although you can work on your mental game as a beginner, its true benefits won't start kicking in until you have a solid grasp on the basic move. No one ever truly masters the mechanical part of sporting clays because of the endless array of variables, such as different targets, trajectories, speeds, backgrounds, and weather. That's why it's always important to practice the fundamentals regardless of level. And it's also important to be patient with yourself when you're in the early stages of developing that skill.

  We are constantly faced with this one: Someone will come to us thinking they have a mental block to get over, when all they really need to do is practice the flashlight drill a couple hundred times or get in the stand and shoot cupcakes on several different presentations. Avoid turning a problem of fundamental mechanics or lack of experience into a mental problem.

- **Do mistakes occur randomly, or do they increase in pressure situations?**
  A technical problem will manifest itself in a wide variety of targets. It could be gun speed, too much or not enough of it. It could be no lateral move, moving up instead of lateral. It could be moving prior to focus. It could be increased grip pressure. It could be that your eyes aren't still. And if they occur randomly, a mechanical correction is usually necessary. But when the problem turns psychological, the mistakes will often occur under pressure, and they will produce a predictable pattern.

Remember when we talked about logs and looking for patterns? Well, this is a big reason why. Look at your log to find the patterns. A few examples would be first station jitters, or last station jitters, having a hard time closing on a good score, misses on the last pair of a stand, or fear of a certain target type or presentation.

- **Do you find yourself having a lot of negative thoughts or feelings during a shoot?**
 If you feel confident and in control of thoughts and emotions during shoots and are still experiencing a plateau or drop in scores, then a simple technical issue is likely the problem. Now, if you feel a sense of panic, if you're pressured or rushed, confused or overloaded by the voice, then your mental game should be addressed.

- **Is the problem affecting one or more aspects of your performance?**
 If there are several things going wrong at the same time, that's a strong sign of a mental game problem. When you are mentally stressed or anxious, it creates muscle tension and interferes with your vision and concentration. So when negative thoughts and emotions control you, a whole host of things can happen: You lose your breakpoints. You make choppy moves. You lose your feel. You check the lead. You go mechanical and conscious, and you listen to everyone but yourself.

When It's All in Your Head

If you determine that the problem is rooted in the mental game, there's no reason to put in a mouth guard and head straight for shock therapy. Bathing in the mighty rivers of wisdom in this book is a good start, but feel free to seek coaching assistance as well. Basically, it's important to understand that "mental game problems" are all a result of negative emotion in the thought process. Revisit the chapters on pre-shot routine, tying up the voice and thought management. At the core, all of this is centered on emotions, how well we control them or how much we let them influence our performance, for better or worse.

Negative emotions obviously induce negative self-talk and make you focus on results, most of all the misses. They leave you in the past, or they take you into the future. You end up overtrying, becoming so preoccupied with shooting a score that you forget about focus, rhythm and trust. Not to mention, negative emotions affect the body by inducing stress and tension.

The mental side of our game is about creating positive or neutral thoughts and picking breakpoints. Not just picking them, but committing to them and believing in them. So when you're practicing, you are always committing to the breakpoint and analyzing your performance based on that commitment, instead of whether or not the target broke. Anyone can handle success! In a game as full of failure as sporting clays, how you react and handle the failure determines the level of your success. Your belief in yourself is what will help you achieve your goals. It's having the feeling, knowing the feeling, and trusting the feeling that leads to success.

Chapter Recap

- A plateau or flatline in scores happens because you've gone as far as you can with the current quality of your move and mental game.

- To move beyond a plateau, something in your move or mental game will have to change.

- Generally defined, a slump is a 10 to 20 percent decrease in score average.

- A slump usually occurs because the shooter has given a lot of emotion to failure.

- Never fear a slump because you will always come out stronger. It's just an indication that something in your game needs to be corrected.

- That something is almost always one little fundamental that has slipped, which has resulted from a loss of feel.

- Feel is the cure for slumps. To regain feel, back off on the difficulty of the targets, avoiding the targets that may be giving you trouble. Shoot simple presentations, looking only for feel.

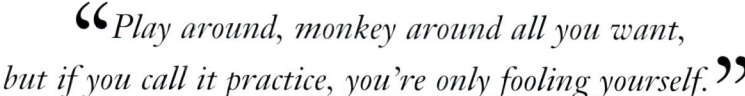

> *"Play around, monkey around all you want, but if you call it practice, you're only fooling yourself."*

CHAPTER TWELVE

HIGH INTENSITY PRACTICE, *with a* PURPOSE

Aside from the feel factor, there is another key ingredient that separates average athletes from the elite. That is practice. Oh sure, you've heard it all before: practice, practice practice—practice makes perfect—practice is everything. We all know great athletes practice hard, and that is obviously true, but what many average athletes don't quite seem to understand is that **great athletes also practice well**. There are many specifics that define that statement, but in general it means three things: they always have a focused purpose for each practice session, they elevate the intensity of their practice to game day quality, and they practice their weaknesses as well as their strengths.

Always Have a Purpose
In our book *If It Ain't Broke, Fix It!* we talked about the difference

Craig Hill's Complete Practice

Practice is a big, important subject. In the beginning, a shooter must relentlessly work on the move and mount. I've spent countless hours working on mine and continue to work on it to this day. Every time I come back to Gil with a problem, he always brings me back to the basic fundamentals of the game. When I have a problem it's typically due to taking one of the fundamentals for granted. It slips a little bit and I get away with it for a while, but eventually it slips far enough away from where it should be that I can't compensate for it and my scores begin to drop off or become inconsistent.

You must continually practice your moves on all targets, improving and embedding them into your subconscious. You can't think about swing mechanics and do this game at a high level. In fact, to do this game at a high level, you better not be thinking at all. Your move to the breakpoint on a scale of 1 to 10 must be a 9 or 10 every time. It must feel smooth and effortless. When you shoot, you must have a total unawareness of the gun. It takes burning a lot of powder to accomplish this. For me it takes 600 to 800 targets a week every week during the season to stay on my game.

I use my pre-shot routine with every practice target I shoot, every one. You must practice enough so that your pre-shot routine is solid and you never have to think about it. It should be automatic. I constantly reinforce my four or five self-talk commands so that they are rapid and clear. This is where most people fall off. They practice their mechanics over and over without practicing their mental game. Use a pre-shot routine and a post-shot routine with every shot. Those routines must be subconscious too.

This game is all about breakpoints and confidence. Nothing builds confidence like being able to break any presentation in three different breakpoints any time you want. Break it five times in a row right off the arm. Break it five times in a row where it's sweet. Break it five times in a row where it's late. You have got to be able to

> do this on all presentations, not just a few. This is the essence of practice. Most people just go and shoot and call it practice. Practice must be disciplined and with a purpose. I always look for and work on my weaknesses. My goal for practice is to have a well-rounded game mechanically and mentally. Practice is where you put it in your subconscious.
>
> Some days I'll just work on the mechanics of my move, always trying to improve my fundamentals, but also with my routine. Other days I'll shoot 100 targets for score and then work on anything that might have given me a problem. Most people are afraid to face a problem or admit that they need help. Not me, I'm always striving to make any weakness a strength by practicing through it. You must own every presentation. The practice field is where you take possession of each and every one of them, one at a time.

between practice and monkeying around. Well, the monkey principle still stands. When your practice sessions lack purpose, it lowers the intensity of the practice and generally leads you to practice your strong points over and over. Play around, monkey around all you want, but if you call it practice, you're only fooling yourself. Just going and shooting the course is not practicing. This is the most common mistake we see among shooters. When NBA players practice, they don't go out and "shoot around" or play a pick-up game. They have a goal and a plan for every session. They break the game into its component parts. NFL players don't play little games of touch football during the week. They practice the component parts of the game each day and play the game once a week. It's the same in any sport, and it's the same for sporting clays. That doesn't mean that practice should lack intensity and fun, but it should always have a goal.

One of the best ways to have a goal for each practice session is by evaluating your shooting log. If you don't have a shooting log to evaluate, you didn't listen in Chapter 2. With a log, the patterns in your shooting will pop off the page, and you'll easily be able to identify problem areas. You should be able to start every session by saying, *Today, I'm going to practice . . .* For example, if you find that you're consistently missing right-to-left crossers, make it your purpose for the next practice session to focus your mechanical training on that trajectory, paying specific attention to playing away from the bird.

The main goal for each session can be anything; it doesn't have to be a component of your mechanical game, but if it is specific and focused, you will have greater success.

Dean Olson On Taking Practice to a Higher Level

You both have shown me what practice really is. People do not give the fundamentals much weight when it comes to the way they practice. They think that shooting a round of a hundred targets is practice. It's not. When I began my journey with OSP, I was shooting a semi-auto. I had purchased an over and under. Gil measured me, but it was going to take four or five months for the gun to be finished. At my fitting, I expressed concern about learning the OSP system with one gun and then switching over to a different gun in mid-season. I will never forget what Gil told me.

He said, "We are not going to train the gun. We are going to train your hands to put the gun where your eyes tell them."

I didn't know what to think. Five months later when the new gun arrived I shot one round of skeet and a couple of rounds of five-stand with it on a Friday afternoon. I shot a tournament on Saturday and Sunday. I was runner-up on Saturday and HOA (high overall) on Sunday, and all the Houston "big dawgs" were there.

It was not the quality of the gun fit that allowed me to perform as well as I did, even though it was perfect. It was the OSP system and coaching on the

Elevate the Intensity

This point cannot be emphasized enough when it comes to practicing in the most effective way. Your intensity and enjoyment in practice should come as close as possible to your intensity and enjoyment on game day. If you don't enjoy practice, you should probably change the way you are practicing, or find an activity that you're truly passionate about and don't mind practicing. This goes back to why you shoot—for yourself or for others.

---

basic fundamentals that allowed me to pick up a new gun and shoot it 75 times and go out and win RU and HOA back to back. Practice is about training your basic fundamental move and mount on all the target trajectories. After each lesson, I was given a certain number of targets to shoot on a certain trajectory in a certain amount of time. I was told to practice my move and mount with the flashlight every day as much as I could. I did what I was told, and in 60 days things began to come together.

My goal for practice had changed from trying to break all the targets to developing a foundation of sound, consistent and subconscious swing mechanics. Rather than teaching me to break certain targets by chasing lead, the OSP system is about learning the importance of the fundamentals and ingraining them into your subconscious. When your fundamentals are sound and subconscious, you are free to totally focus on the targets. I continue to be amazed when I go back to Gil or Vicki with a problem. Regardless of what I perceive it to be, it is always a breakdown in the basic fundamentals of the move.

Practice for me in the beginning was about building the foundation. It has evolved into using the foundation I have built the most efficient way possible to eliminate any and all excess movement during the shot. Efficiency in the move increases your ability to maintain focus on the targets when they are in the air. The consistency of your move allows you to not have to think about swing mechanics when the targets are in the air. You can't think and shoot, and that is one of the basic fundamentals of the OSP system.

If you really love shooting, but aren't fond of practice, we can help. The first thing you can do is to bring more intensity to practice. The reason that you love shooting on game day is because of the intensity, right? Well, you are the one who creates that intensity in your own mind; it's self-created, so create it in practice. If you can make yourself salivate when you visualize peeling an orange, you can make yourself feel like you're in a tournament even when it's practice. We tell our students that practice is not just breaking targets, it's making every shot count like you had to have it to win.

Our friend Craig Hill puts it this way: "You've got to bring your practice game to the tournament. You will never shoot better on game day than you do in practice." We have yet to see a shooter who does, but if you have a great practice game, you'll have a much better chance at success when you bring it to the tournament. One thing Craig recommends to elevate the intensity is to tell yourself, *this shot is for a million dollars* when you want to kick it up a notch. Or if you have a practice partner, make a gentleman's bet. When you get to the last pair, say it out loud. These types of things will help to create that atmosphere.

The other benefit of practicing like it's game day is that you become more accustomed to the way it feels when you're at a tournament. Most everyone deals with the challenge of pressure at tournaments, but if you practice like it's game day, then the tournament is just another practice day. The pressure will diminish.

Practice Weaknesses

This is something we see a lot in beginning and intermediate shooters. They will conquer a particular trajectory and then continue to practice it more than any other presentation because they know they can hit it.

When elite shooters practice, they don't just go out and shoot a flat of ammo. They're looking for weaknesses in their game, and they're determined to exploit those weaknesses and turn them into strengths. If they have a nemesis target, they're working on that target, shooting it in different breakpoints and from different distances. This is what we recommend for each practice session: look to eliminate your weaknesses. That isn't to say that you shouldn't move on if you miss six or eight in a row on any given target. If that's the case, we'd recommend taking a break, shooting some different targets for a while before coming back. If the trajectory is still perplexing you, find a qualified coach who can help.

The problem with continuing to miss over and over on a given target is that you begin to program the misses in your mind. So there is a certain balance you want to achieve. It's not helpful to be so afraid to miss that you stick with shooting feel-good targets you know you can hit and never practice your weaknesses, but if you find yourself missing over and over again, take a break or seek help.

Like we said in the last chapter, there is a time to shoot cupcakes, but it's one thing to back off on difficulty when looking to regain more feel during a slump, and it's another to stick with one trajectory just because it's more comfortable.

There should be some kind of single target trajectory practice during each practice session where you nitpick the move, but if it's always the one trajectory you're best at, you're setting up for a long plateau.

Frequency and Quality, Not Quantity
One more general comment we'd like to make about practice before we move on to specifics. Practicing smart, practicing well, and practicing often is much more effective than shooting tons of targets for hours on end with no plan or intensity. We have

found that a practice schedule leaning toward shorter, higher-quality sessions more often produces better results than long sessions every once in a while. When you go out and shoot a massive volume of bullets once a week or once every other week, there will be a point in that session where you're just not retaining any more. If you keep shooting bullets, it won't do any good. But if you commit yourself to a shorter session two or three times a week and a few minutes of gun mount practice with visualization every day, you will retain more and continue to increase your skill level.

Move Training vs. Performance Practice

We're going to get into some specific practice regimens we recommend, but we want to say this first: We encourage you to seek your own level of how much practice is enough and what kind of practice works best for you. The ratios we are about to suggest are general guidelines that have been successful for our students, but we're not all clones, so there will be some variations. Start with these and see how they work, but we always recommend experimentation.

In our system, we break practice into two categories. We usually call one "training" and the other "practice," but for the sake of clarity, we'll give them more specific names here. How about "Move Training" versus "Performance Practice."

Move training is getting consciously involved with changes in your move on a specific target. An example would be paying particular attention to bringing the gun all the way to your cheek, or concentrating on letting the bird come to you (playing away). If you're working on a problem target or a new move, that is move training. It means you're deliberately thinking about the move, trying to groove it and ingrain it in your subconscious. So there will be some thought toward mechanics.

Obviously, new shooters will be spending a lot of time on move training, but there should be some move training in every one of your sessions, regardless of level.

Performance practice, on the other hand, is training your overall game. It's learning to more fully commit to the breakpoint, trusting the move, making the routine perfect, building confidence. It's shooting stations of five pairs in a row, just like you would in a tournament. This is practicing like it's game day, where that intensity thing comes into play. There should be little, if any, mechanical thought. Trusting the routine and the plan is critical during performance practice. The main objectives are getting connected to each and every target through feel, and trusting the subconscious to take the shot.

There should also be some performance practice during every one of your sessions. In fact, one of the most frequent inefficiencies we see in shooters' practice routines is that they go out and do move training all the time but never any performance practice. They never practice like it's game day. This type of practice is how you get better at shooting "out of your mind," so you can see the correlation. If most shooters don't practice feel, if they never practice techniques to get them "out of mind," then most shooters will never have feel during competition. That's why we harp on feel, and it's why we harp on performance practice. Most shooters seem to believe that move training is the only way to practice.

Does that mean we want everyone to shoot stations of five pairs in a row for the majority of every session at the range? No. You'll train the move and practice performance in different amounts based on several things: your current performance plateau, when your next tournament is scheduled, or if you're trying to implement something new into your game.

Practice Based on Plateaus

We talked about the plateaus in the last chapter. As promised, here is a general breakdown of what we would practice at each step of the plateau. These averages should be the scores you average in tournaments, not practice. And keep in mind that this is not pre-tournament practice. This is what you'll want to practice after a tournament, based on your average.

- We're going to start at 65. Shooters below this level should be devoting all of their time to the flashlight drill exercises, single target move training, and maybe some visualization with the gun in their hands. Once you're around the 65 mark, you should be move training about 80 percent of the time and practicing performance about 20 percent. That means devoting 80 percent of your time on single targets and 20 percent on report pairs or true pairs. The reason is that at this level, it isn't the pairs that are killing you, it's the lack of a good subconscious move. Work on the crossing move in particular. Continue to use the flashlight drill; always do this, but pay special attention to it here. Stay away from targets that are fast at this point.

- Now let's go to 72. Here, we would tell you to do move training 70 percent of the time and performance practice 30 percent. Your move still isn't subconscious enough, although it's improving, so you are still grooving the fundamentals. Introduce quartering birds into your move regimen. The flashlight drill is great for this presentation, too.

- At 75, the targets should still be fairly slow and close, but the move training should be bumped down to 60 percent and the performance practice bumped up to 40 percent. This is where commitment to the breakpoint becomes a critical aspect to focus on. A quick word about performance practice, shooting pairs like you would in a tournament: If you don't have the luxury of shooting ten different stations in a row for whatever reason, you can shoot the same station over and over again. Just change the breakpoints, change the pattern with which you shoot the birds, and move your own shooting position if it's possible to do so safely.

- When you get to 78, trusting the breakpoint is essential, as is developing a stronger routine. Your setup and visualization of the targets upon setup should be a subconscious function, or very close to it. This is also the 50-50 point, where half your time is now devoted to performance practice and shooting pairs, while half is still move training.

    It's around this time that we find many shooters have a strong urge to rush through the move training to get to pairs. They're almost shooting 80, man, they don't need to worry so much about the fundamentals. Besides, pairs are more fun. It's easy to fall into that trap, but we would caution against hazing over the move training. Devote your full attention and energy to these targets, and make your fundamental move the highest quality possible. Keep pushing the curve.

- Let's move on to the 82 plateau. Here your performance practice should begin to slightly dominate your move training. A ratio of about 60 percent performance to 40 percent move is a good place to start. Your move here is probably an 8 or an 8.5 out of 10. Now it's important to look at your tournament scores and isolate that one move that is your weakest move so you're training on your weakest move the most. And even during your move training, you are looking for feel and focus more than mechanics.

- At 84, it's important to further define your routine, make it more subconscious, and further define your weaknesses. Look for feel and trust more than anything else. We're sure you're catching on to the pattern by now, and already know that the ratio is 30 percent move training and 70 percent performance practice. It's all about scoring now. You have to learn to love scoring ugly on game day, rejecting mechanical thoughts, and trusting the move that you bring to every tournament. Intensity in practice is huge.

- When you hit the 86 average, feel is of utter importance, and that is attained by tying the voice up in the breakpoint. Your mental game is going to decide where you go from here. The move training is now at 20 percent, and game-day simulating performance practice is 80 percent. You are shooting pairs, 5 times in a row, and you're only happy if you break them 5 times in a row in the breakpoints. Your weaknesses are easier to isolate because there are fewer of them, but once you find one, go after it. Don't say, "Well, if I can't break it there, I can always break it in that other spot." Increase your confidence in breaking it anywhere.

> **Bending the Ratios**
> One quick word on these ratios: You can still be flexible with them. If we tell you to shoot a 60/40 ratio, it's fine if you want to shoot 50/50 or 70/30 based on what works for you. The important thing to understand is that the higher your score plateau gets, the more you should begin focusing on performance practice. But remember to always train a basic move in every session, regardless of score.

- It's still 20 percent move training and 80 percent performance practice when you're averaging 88. You have terrific fundamentals, but at this point, it's a lot easier for them to slip than it is for them to improve; that's why we stick to around 20 percent move training. Even during that move training though, you are now more interested in feel than mechanics, especially if you're not implementing a change or trying something new you learned in a lesson. This is also the plateau where you can start working on more difficult birds on a routine basis— more difficult meaning 35 to 55 yards; fast, driving birds; birds that make quick transitions; and scenarios like high tower targets. (For clarity, an example of a bird in quick transition is a blazing crosser that starts as an incomer, transitions into a crosser and ends as an outgoer). Maybe one out of every three sessions you should give significant attention to more difficult birds. You've probably already started shooting birds like these, which is okay, but you don't really need to start shooting them until this point. It's still the ones you should have hit that are hurting you.

- When you hit a 92 average, the first thing you should do is look back at all you have accomplished. Congratulations are in order. There is no way you've reached this point without learning to tie the voice up, and you now know what it's like to have a connection to a target through feel—to have a move so in sync with the targets that you know they're dead before you pull the trigger. So take a minute to gain a little perspective.

Done?

Okay, well, we still advocate an 80 percent performance practice and 20 percent move training regimen. At every practice session you will still train on one specific move for a certain percentage of the time.

When you average in the 90s, your mental game takes center stage, as does your plan. You've got to have boundless trust—boundless trust in your ability to connect with a target through feel and boundless trust in your subconscious to carry out the shot without mechanical instruction. You must also realize that it's not the opponent you're seeking to beat—it's the course.

Always an Exception

There are two exceptions to the ratios we've set out. The first is one we've already talked about, practice during slumps. Your practice during slumps should fall back to 100 percent fundamentals, or move training, but with all your attention focused on gaining feel. So it's a bit of a combination of both types. You are shooting fluffy single targets, but you aren't concerned with mechanics. You want the feel you get in performance practice combined with the simplicity of move training. We're talking "See Dick Run, First Grade Reader" targets—no pairs.

The other exception to the ratio is when you've learned something new and want to ingrain it, especially after a lesson. This is also a good time to go to a 100 percent move training regimen. The only difference from this and the practice during a slump or when a problem arises is that you can focus more on the mechanics. If it's a new addition to your move, you'll have to think mechanics. Let's say you just came for a lesson on flying rabbits. We found that your lateral move to the breakpoint wasn't strong enough. The rabbit was overrunning the muzzles. So we tweaked your move during the lesson and asked you to practice it that way so it will become subconscious.

When you go back to your next couple of practice sessions, you can set up and practice the flying rabbit 100 percent of the time, consciously aware of getting that muzzle out in front of the bird. When it gets to the point that you don't have to think about it, you know it's in your subconscious database, and you can go back to your normal ratio.

Practice Ratios Before a Tournament
We change the ratios for practice sessions one or two weeks before a tournament. As you see how they differ from normal sessions, you might pick up on why. If not, we'll tell you at the end.
- At a 65 average, a pre-tournament practice session should be 40 percent move training and 60 percent performance practice. That contrasts with 80 percent move training and 20 percent

performance practice in a normal session. So you're cutting back mechanical training on singles and increasing the number of pairs. You're focusing on tempo and set-up, and you're working on weaknesses. The pairs, however, should not be difficult.

- At 72–75, the ratio is 20 percent move training to 80 percent performance practice (instead of 60/40). Still, make sure the pairs are easy, and constantly work on your weaknesses. Try report pairs and true pairs, and refrain from shooting anything outside of 30 yards. At a 75 score plateau, it isn't the 40-yard crossers that are going to beat you in your class. It's the easy ones you let go that get you!
- A shooter with a 78 average should practice move training 15 percent of the time and performance practice 85 percent during a pre-tournament session. Work on your routine and making sure your eyes are still before you call pull. And constantly work on one particular move that you perceive as a weakness, making it a strength.
- At 82, the ratio stays the same: 15 percent move, 85 percent performance. Even at this level you want to stay with easy pairs, working on tempo, trust, and routine. Incorporate as much visualization as possible. You've probably never heard this from us before, but during that 15 percent move practice, work on your weakest move.
- Instead of the 30/70 ratio in a normal session for the 84 average, the pre-tournament ratio should be closer to 10 percent move training and 90 percent performance practice. It's fine to work on a few medium difficulty pairs, but continue focus on routine and tempo. The more visualization and intensity you can include, the better. Just like it's game day, everything is serious, everything is with a routine. It's breakpoint one, breakpoint two, back to breakpoint one, routine … call pull, and break the pair.

- The same goes for an 86 average: it's 10 percent move, 90 percent performance. Be satisfied only when you run 10 straight in the same breakpoints every time. Make sure your

---

Ron Outruns His Goals

Ron Schaffer is a student who is probably one of the strongest competitors we've ever seen. He had racked up quite a few accomplishments and accolades in this sport but hit a plateau that he couldn't seem to get beyond. Ron told us that he'd shot so many tournaments that he was tired, and he wasn't practicing much because practice had become boring. That was a red flag. We knew that Ron loved the sport, so we asked him about his goals. He said, "Well, you know, I don't really have one." So we asked: "What were your first goals?"

"I was in E class and my first goal was to get to C, and then my next goal was to get from C to A," he said. "I did that last year, and this year I'm in AA, but I'm experiencing very erratic performance."

We talked some more and discussed that it's easier to move up in the classes as an E or C shooter when you have that as a general goal, but as a AA shooter, the goal should become more specific. We felt that Ron had outrun his goal of reaching A class and didn't really set a new goal afterward. With no specific goal, his practice had become boring because there was really nothing to work toward. For the last few years on the "Coaching Hour," we've talked about how you have to bring your practice level to a higher quality in order for you to compete on a higher level, and that was what we discussed with Ron.

It took him a while to commit to a new goal, but he did; it was to make the SuperVet All-American Team. Although it was a much bigger goal than he ever expected to make way back in E class, he eventually came to believe in it. And when belief happens, it's the strongest power a person can wield. It's tough to overcome a plateau if you aren't looking up, confident in the path you see ahead. That's what happened with Ron. With a clear path ahead, he achieved his goal and became captain of the All-American Super Vet Team!

practice is held at tournament intensity. It might also be a good idea to run through your performance practice without a warm-up, to get used to that situation that can sometimes occur in tournaments. Use the visualization technique (page 66) instead.

- At a score plateau of 88, the ratio is the same. (It'll be the same for the next one, too). There should still be some time devoted to move training, but the 90 percent majority should be performance practice on pairs. The closer the tournament gets, the easier the pairs should be, although if you're a few weeks out as an 86, 88, or 92 shooter, try some more difficult pairs, but leave them behind if you don't run them. Then, during your 10 percent move training, practice on the ones you missed.
- The 10/90 ratio still stands even when you're at the 90-plus plateau. Work on the rhythm of the station, feeling the lateral move to the breakpoint, trusting your routine and your move. It's all focus and trust in practice, just like it is on game day. Still, don't neglect the 10 percent move training. Focus on feel, but do it while concentrating on your weakest move.

Now, if you didn't pick up on it, the reason we pump up the performance practice over move training before a tournament is to get you more in the game day mindset, where feel and focus reign over mechanical thoughts. Make the sessions as intense as possible to see how well you can tie up the voice. Try to create in your mind the same pressures that you will feel on the day of the tournament. This type of preparation will make you feel like you've already been there when the day actually comes.

Practicing With a Partner

In general, we recommend practicing alone for a big chunk of your practice sessions. It helps to eliminate as many distractions as possible. However, some of our students, especially those below the AA or Master Class, have really found benefits in bringing along a partner who speaks the same language. By that we mean someone who understands the concept of connecting to a target through feel, letting the bird come to the gun, tying up the voice with the breakpoint, etc. Having an objective observer who knows what to look for and understands coaching feel can be a great blessing. When you do practice with a partner, we've found that it's best to practice with someone who is at a similar score average or higher.

If you're a AA or Master Class shooter, the most productive practice will probably be accomplished in solitude, because when you're in the shootoff arena, you're gonna be all by your lonesome.

In closing, we'll leave you with some quotes about practice, because everybody likes quotes. Here's one we read a few years ago that we'll never forget. "My opponents may outscore me, but they will never outwork me." Tiger Woods said that, and it is a great insight into the practice mindset of an elite athlete. We would add something, though. Not only is it a great goal to practice the hardest, it's an even better one to practice the smartest. If your opponents never outwork you or practice smarter than you or practice with a higher quality and intensity, you will be very tough to outshoot.

Here's one more: "Every great shot that you hit, you must have already done many times in practice." That one was Martina Navratilova, and we agree completely. And we think it goes not only for every great shot, but for every great performance. If your practice performances are exceptional, you're increasing the probability that your tournament performances will be the same. Like just about everything else in life, if you're not enjoying it, you're probably not doing it the right way.

Chapter Recap

- Practicing well is just as important as practicing hard.

- The first step to quality practice is to have a purpose for each session.

- The next step is to elevate the intensity of your practice by bringing a tournament mindset to each practice.

- Practicing your weaknesses is extremely important for quality practice. Shoot the targets that are your weak spot, but move on if you continue to miss a certain presentation.

- Shooters who practice well and practice often will experience greater success than shooters who practice without a plan or who shoot tons of targets with no intensity.

- We break practice into two types: move training and performance practice. Move training is about being consciously involved in making changes to your fundamentals. Performance practice is shooting stations of five pairs in a row, just like game day, forgetting mechanics, concentrating on feel and the overall game.

- There are specific ratios of performance practice versus move training that we recommend based on score plateaus. Look them up.

- The ratios will change slightly when the practice sessions are just before a tournament.

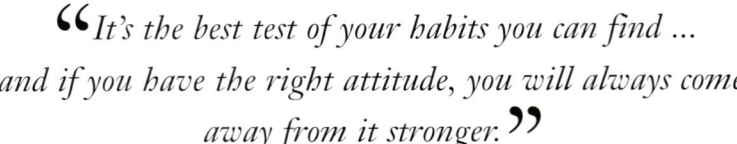

"It's the best test of your habits you can find ... and if you have the right attitude, you will always come away from it stronger."

CHAPTER THIRTEEN

TOURNAMENT SHOOTING

Everything seems to have a bit more tang on tournament day. If you've competed in one, you know this. The sun seems brighter, the guns seem to pop a bit louder, and if it's raining, well, it seems ... wetter. (That's right, wetter.) What we're trying to say is, it all feels more alive, including that knot of muscle beating in your chest. And isn't that the reason we love it? Isn't that the point? It could be that we do these things just out of a desire for better circulation. Or maybe it's the cash prizes, but whether you do it for love or money, shooting in a tournament is an exceptional experience.

If this is new territory for you, there are hundreds if not thousands of clays sports tournaments held every year in just about every state. The National Sporting Clays Association and National Skeet Shooting Association (www.nssa-nsca.com) have lists of all the club tournaments available throughout the country. The Amateur Trapshooting Association (www.shootata.com)

does as well. The competition ranges from beginners and casual shooters to serious competitors and professionals.

We love tournaments, we love coaching tournament shooters, and we'd recommend tournaments to anyone with a passion for this game. Is it a good idea to work on developing solid fundamentals first, to wait until you have confidence in the six basic trajectories? Absolutely. In fact, shooting a tournament too early in the year is something we caution beginning shooters against. But if you've got a solid grasp of the fundamentals, are thinking about trying your hand at a tournament, and need a little nudge, consider us the nudgers. It's the best test of your habits you can find, it's an exciting atmosphere with a lot of camaraderie, and if you have the right attitude, you will always come away from it stronger. Practicing and never competing is like doing the tango by yourself, or playing both sides of the chessboard. It's just never quite as much fun solo.

Picking Your Tournaments

When you've committed to developing as a tournament shooter, our first advice is to plan out your year at the end of the off-season. Yes, the plan will change, but the important thing is to pick a tournament or tournaments where you want to peak. (We recommend taking a break from clay target shooting during the winter, which is the typical off-season for most tournament shooters.) Based on your commitment to the game, if three big shoots is all you'll be able to shoot in a year, pick one that is the most important to you. If you'll hit five big shoots, pick two where you'd like to peak. If it's ten tournaments, pick three to five. That's not to say you don't have a goal to shoot well at all the tournaments you attend, but by picking three to five, you are committing yourself to the highest level of practice and preparation possible for those specific shoots. The goal is to create and experience the deepest zone you can. As for timing, it makes sense to schedule those important events during a period when there won't be a lot of other draws on your time. Try to avoid those times when you know you'll have a lot of responsibilities at work or at home, so you can devote a large chunk of time to practice and preparation.

You'll still practice and prepare for the shoots that you haven't designated as your "majors," but you'll also have some flexibility. If you're thinking of trying some new preparations or routines, maybe some new concentration techniques, a smaller tournament is a great time to experiment. Find out what it takes for you to perform well at the smaller shoots, and bring that knowledge to the few shoots you've targeted for the best of your best performances. Your ability to create peak performances is tied to how much you experiment at these smaller tournaments. And if you have a few tournaments where it's all right for you to experiment, you won't beat yourself up if the performance isn't your best.

But just be aware that you won't be able to shoot 20 to 25 tournaments a year with proper preparation and still have a job and a family life. There are other things that will take priority, and mapping out your year is recognizing this. Pick a few tournaments where the goal is not to win (gasp!) but simply to go out and have some fun, meet some folks, and relax. So at the beginning of the year, take a look at your work and family schedules, and map your shooting schedule around those. Make a rough training schedule, and keep in mind that a lot of intermediate and advanced shooters actually over-train just before a big tournament. If you'll start training for your scheduled peak performances three weeks ahead of time based on your weaknesses at the last small tournament, you'll be ready to peak.

When to Travel

For shooters who are already shooting local tournaments and are unable to break consistently into the 90s despite solid fundamentals and a strong mental game, it may be time to take your game on the road. If your schedule permits it, we've found that traveling to big shoots at different courses around the country is often that last piece of the puzzle that helps good shooters become great shooters. The more you expose yourself to different tournament experiences of greater intensity, the stronger your game will get. There's something about hopping on an airplane or making that long drive, strapping a number on your back and competing alongside hundreds of other shooters that forges your game to a sharper point.

Tournament Practice

We talked about tournament practice in the last chapter but there are a few things we'd like to reiterate. Overall, your pre-tournament practice should be designed to build confidence, trust in your pre-shot routine, and feel. So shooting very fast or very long targets is not recommended. Shoot easy pairs. Practice staying in a consistent rhythm, and stay focused on breakpoint. Shoot everything with a pre-shot routine. Maintain game day intensity as you move from presentation to presentation, shooting five or six pairs in a row in the same spot. It's commitment to the breakpoint that's going to keep the voice out.

The other thing we recommend is putting the gun down two to three days before a tournament. In our opinion, practicing right up to the day of the tournament is a product of fear—it's giving in to the voice. Believe that you can do it. Believe that you're ready. We've seen plenty of people who are crackerjack shots go out and shoot 400 targets just before the tournament. By the time the tournament starts, they're no longer crackerjack shots; they're wasted.

If you have a few weeks of committed practice available, take the time to shoot 100 targets like you would on game day, then focus on your weakest presentations. If you're feeling strong, throw in a few targets that would rate as mid to high difficulty for you. Set up the atmosphere of competition during practice, so there is a bit more pressure.

If time is short, concentrate on easy pairs. If time is even shorter and you really have to skimp on field practice, make it a point to have that gun in your hands every night, working on visualization with feel. If you only have one solid practice session before a tournament, concentrate on getting a felt connection to that target. Make it feel like it's nothing more than an extension of you. In your pre-shot routine, really fortify that moment where you keep your eyes still before calling for the bird. We've seen plenty of shooters perform very well at a tournament even though they didn't get as much range time as they would have liked, but they DID have the gun in their hands every night, they DID visualize, and they DID concentrate on getting a felt connection to the targets.

Preparation Tips

The most important thing we're going to tell you about shooting tournaments on the road is the same thing your momma told you for years: go to bed. Listen to your momma. We have been traveling to teach and shoot for a long time now, and lack of proper sleep is the one thing we can't afford. We can get by for a few days with a little slacking on diet and exercise, but the same relaxed, deep sleep that we get at home is essential. And we know from talking to our students and other shooters that we're not alone. If you want to perform to your highest potential, you must be well rested and alert.

The perfect time to find out what it takes for you to achieve that state is during those "experimental" tournaments that we talked about before. It's a good idea to bring your own pillow from home if you can. If you're traveling across two time zones to shoot in a tournament, pre-acclimate your body by going to bed and waking up at the same hour you'll need to for the tournament time zone, but do so a few days before you leave home.

Although there is a little room for error with proper diet and nutrition, we would admonish you to do all that you can to keep your diet on the road the same as it would be at home. (Hopefully you have a decent diet at home.) What we typically see is that most people eat a big breakfast on the road, and they don't normally do that. They also tend to indulge themselves a bit more when they're eating out, rather than eating home-cooked meals. We, ourselves, have never done this, so that's why we said "they."

Also, as we said in the previous chapter, we recommend cutting off practice one or two days prior to leaving for a tournament on the road. For a local shoot, the last practice session can be two days prior to the shoot. If you've prepared properly, this will be a big advantage. Keep your body in good shape and eat right, but know that you're ready to shoot.

Oh, and one last thing: When you're traveling and expect to be competitive, we recommend that you avoid shooting too many events at one tournament. If you're just going to have fun and meet people, shoot everything there. But if you are serious about having a solid performance, focus on one or two events where you'd like to shoot the best you possibly can.

Previewing the Course

We're not going to push you either way when it comes to previewing a tournament course. Some of our shooters like to do it if they have the opportunity, while other shooters like to analyze it fresh. The case for previewing a course is that it allows you to watch good shooters go through the stations and see if there are any mistakes you can learn from. It also allows you more time to find hidden machines and walk around the traps to survey the terrain like a golfer before a putt. Target setters often use the terrain as an illusion. Some shooters like to do a quick preview mainly as preparation for choke changes, so they know what they've got coming up. Also, some have mentioned that a preview the day before sometimes makes long presentations look shorter the second time you see them.

The case against previewing is based on the fact that you might not get to preview some tournament courses. If that happens and it causes you anxiety, it should be a red flag. We are fine with previewing as long as it doesn't supercede your ability to shoot the course cold. Also, you should understand that when you're shooting a course cold, you have as much time as you need to analyze the presentation. Ask for your look pair. There's no need to rush.

Competing the Weekend Before

When it comes to major tournaments—those you have picked for peak performance—we think shooting a smaller tournament the weekend before is only advisable if you're a fairly seasoned shooter. If you're an E or D class shooter, just beginning to develop your routine, it's probably not the best idea to shoot a tournament the weekend before Nationals or the U.S. Open. Focus instead on practicing well, working on the routine, shooting ten in a row on easy pairs. It's all about confidence. But AA and Master shooters with the ability to leave poor performances behind them will probably go ahead and shoot the smaller tournament. They have been seasoned to the point where they can look at the smaller tournament as nothing more than a practice session and won't let a high or low score affect their mindset for the big tournament.

Reading Targets

This is a huge subject because the variety of targets in sporting clays is endless. We're not going to cover every presentation we've seen, but we will dole out some of the general wisdom we've gained on reading targets. We've already covered some ground in Chapter 13 of our book, *If It Ain't Broke, Fix It!* and in our DVD, *Strategy and How to Play the Game*. Here we'll get to some advice we've gleaned from our years of experience and from some of the best target setters in the sport.

- Watch targets all the way to the ground. This is rule number one. When you're watching a "look" pair, follow the target all the way to the ground. We've probably said it before, but as Vicki likes to say, "The fact that we get paid to repeat ourselves is called job security, baby." On true pairs, one tip for getting a clear idea of the speed and line relationship is to look between the birds when they are both in the air, and trace the lines out of your periphery. It is of great advantage to know their entry point, crossing points, which one is high, which one is low, which one is fast and which one is slow. You know? This makes your plan for the pair more obvious and easier to believe in. And wherever you decide to break the first target, you instantly know where to look for and break the second. (This is covered in more detail in our DVD, *Strategy and How to Play the Game*.)
- Walk around the presentation. It's a good idea to walk down the pathway and see if you can find traps that are hidden behind bushes or trees. Have a look at the presentation from as many different angles as possible to get an accurate reading.
- Always ask the trapper what the targets are: standard and a midi? Two standards? A rabbit thrown in the air? Upside down bateau? Expert target setters can use different types of targets to deceive the eyes.

- Get in the mindset of a target setter. There are several things that many target setters like to do on a regular basis. Here are some of the most common:

    They will try to set a wide distance between targets. Setters do this so that shooters who try to take the targets where they are "easiest" will have a very difficult time of it. The way to combat this is by learning to break the targets in many different spots. If you can move breakpoints, you can make targets easier by keeping the breakpoints together.

    They will throw a flat bird with a curling bird, or a fast bird with a slow bird. Target setters will try to mix up the rhythm and lines in a pair as much as possible. They do this because they know that most shooters have only one "speed" of move. The way to combat this is by moving at the same speed of each bird, the method we teach to all of our students.

    They will use topography to fool the eye. Many target setters are excellent at throwing a target over sloped ground at the same angle so that the target looks like it's moving perfectly horizontal, with barely any curve, when in reality it's got a great deal of curl. Viewing the presentation from many different angles helps. So does holding your gun parallel to the ground and looking at the birds over that level surface.

    They will throw targets with a mix in lead and line. This means throwing something with a lot of lead, like a long, fast crosser, with something that takes very little, like a simple quartering bird or a dying crosser.

- Listen to your gut. When your intuition is telling you to break a target in a different way, using a different breakpoint than most other shooters, go with it. That gut reaction is based on your ability and training, so make your own plan and stick to it. If it doesn't work, change it, but we think you'll be surprised how often it's right.

Game Day

You've practiced well for the last month, eliminating the weaknesses in your game by looking for patterns in your shooting log. You've prepared with visualization and practically feel like you've already won the tournament several times. You've been eating right, getting decent exercise, and making sure you're well hydrated and well rested. You understand that you're about to discover how good your habits are, which ones are better than others, and nothing more. You know that the other shooters are there to help push you to perform to the best of your abilities, which is the original intention of all competition. Your mind is quiet and your body is relaxed, and the warm feeling of excitement is in your chest. It's game day, boys and girls. Go have fun.

The best advice we have for tournament day is to focus on what you can control. That's what "bringing your practice to game day" is all about. You can control your emotions, your pre-shot and correction routines, your move and mount, and what you focus on during a shot. You can set your goal to be passionately consumed with the shot at hand and nothing else. Among many, many other things you can't control, here are a few: the target presentation, the weather, your squad mates, targets in the past, targets in the future, the efficiency of the tournament, targets you miss, how many targets your competitors hit, and *the scoreboard*. Why focus on any of these things when you have absolutely no control over them?

We highlighted the scoreboard because so many shooters think about this during game day. Our advice is to simply stay away from the scoreboard until you have fired your last shot on the last day of the tournament. Checking your score before that is simply a huge invitation to the voice to come in and make you overconfident or to beat you up. Your thoughts should be so tied up in the present, with making the plan and shooting the plan, that you have almost no idea what your score is. Yes, you'll know if you're in the hunt, but staying away from the scoreboard gives some assistance in focusing only on the things you can control.

Flatline your emotions through non-judgmental thinking. Whatever happens, accept it, learn from it, and move on. Like Mark Twain said: "The inability to forget is infinitely more devastating than the inability to remember." Know that it only takes one thought to do your best or your worst. So concentrate on the positive things. Counteract every negative comment someone makes with something positive: "Man, the sun is going to be in our eyes on this course." *"I'm comfortable breaking the targets anywhere, so I can take the sun out of the game."*

Trust your feel. Trust your subconscious to perform the way you've trained it. Let go of all thoughts of mechanics.

Women assertive; men calm. In general, we've found that women are able to attain a focused and relaxed state of concentration when they put themselves in an aggressive or assertive mindset. For most men, it's the opposite: a calm, tranquil frame of mind usually facilitates the zone more easily.

Understand that you can create your own zone before the tournament ever starts or at any time during the tournament. You can do what it takes to put yourself in that upward spiral by becoming interested and staying neutral emotionally. Put yourself in a state of relaxed concentration. Welcome that tingle of excitement in your chest. It's great to be excited, but realize that you should relax and let things happen as they will. Use that excitement in a positive way instead of turning it over to fear and doubt.

Stick to your plan regarding breakpoints. Success without a plan is luck. Read the targets, make your plan, believe it, and commit to it. You know how to tie up the voice in the breakpoint. The deeper in the plan you are, the deeper in your zone you become. As that happens, anxiety, doubt, and fear will fade away.

Yes, there is some luck involved in winning performances. But just be aware that having a goal and having a plan to achieve the goal allows you to take full advantage of whatever luck comes your way. And if you're not ready to make that good score, if you're not all there, all the luck in the world won't help you get there.

Avoid watching more targets than you need to. Once you've analyzed a presentation and feel confident in your plan, give your eyes a break and go get involved in some of Gil Ash's Minutia. Watching the targets of every other shooter is a waste of your focus.

If you experience the first station jitters, visualize shooting two stations before you step up to the first one. When you're done, it will no longer be the first one.

When you feel yourself starting to lose your calm, slow everything down. Anxiety will make you speed up without it even registering. So concentrate on slowing down. Talk slower, walk slower. If you're driving a Clays Car, get somebody else to drive and walk to the next station. Everything you touch, touch it softly. Relax your jaw, your neck and your shoulders. Equalize your grip pressure by squeezing the gun hard for three seconds and then relaxing completely before coming back to neutral.

Resistance is futile. When you are closing on a great score, you will know it. Instead of resisting the thought, go ahead and acknowledge it, and then move on. Everyone recognizes that it's a huge challenge to refrain from going mechanical when you're in the hunt and you're on the last few stations. We think the cure is to just stay true to the breakpoint.

Smile. There's nothing better for tension than a smile. It will also help you slow down and remember that you're playing a game. This ain't Vietnam. You're just playing Cowboys and Indians.

It's not the perceived difficulty of the targets that matters, it's how you play them. It matters less who wins or loses; it matters more who you become.

Handling the Pressure

We talk a lot about tournaments on our monthly call-in "Coaching Hour." In September 2002, the question came up regarding how great shooters handle tournament pressure. The responses were great, and we'd like to include a few clips of that transcript here.

Craig: What I've found more than anything, the more you put yourself in the situations like that, each time is a little different, that you learn something from being in the position to win. Each time it's a different anxiety. I think it's a learning experience, and the more times you do it, the more times you know what's coming. What your body is going to do or what you're going to feel. I think the more you do it, you just figure it out along the way. Me, I try to make sure I get a good night's rest, I eat good, and try to stay hydrated.

I like to feel calm, and what makes me feel calm is knowing that I'm prepared with my gear and my breakfast, all that stuff. I just get tied up in the details and making sure things are just perfect along the way. I know I'm ready to shoot, but I just get tied up in making sure everything is right.

Nathan: I have no routines to wake up in the morning to keep the pressure off. All I do is keep my mind off of it. I stay away from it. Hang around with friends, do anything but put myself out on that course. Because I know that I've trained hard enough. I know that I'm a good shooter. I know that whatever I do that day, I'm going to be in the hunt.

Craig: Well, it's funny we're talking about this, because the last time I saw Dan Carlisle I asked him the same question. I said, "What do you do?" Because I ask everybody. And we were talking about not going into the future, not thinking about winning. You know, how do you not think about the finish line and about getting your damn trophy when you're three targets from getting it? And Dan's answer was, "Go ahead and go there, think about winning it, but then come back to the cage, and say, 'Okay, now I've got to break these ten to do it.'

So you can go there and then come back so you don't pinball between thoughts like, what if I win? Well, don't think about winning. But if I just hit this. Oh, don't think that. You have to get your mind calm. Go ahead and go there but then come back and find the calm.

Gil: Years ago when Vicki and I

were traveling and shooting, we had a friend named Arnie Townley, and he traveled with John Kruger quite a bit. One day I asked Arnie, "What does John do when he gets up in the morning before a shoot?"

And he said, "You won't believe me."

I said: "No, what?"

He replied, "He has to watch the Smurfs in the morning on TV."

And that's what he does. He just gets his mind off the game and wrapped up in something silly like a cartoon, and just relaxes, and when he goes out, he's ready to shoot. So there are a lot of different ways that people ready themselves.

Bob: It's all the same, and Craig said it before: Bring your practice to game day. That's what elite athletes worldwide do.

Gil: You can't not think about the fact that you're in the hunt if you're in the hunt. You know you're in the hunt. And the more you resist it, the more the voice is going to get in. The louder the voice is going to scream. But what you can do is let the thought in, and then focus on something else. You can control the thought in the cage two to three seconds at a time, when you're in your routine and you're shooting the targets.

The "Coaching Hour" CDs are available through our website, www.ospschool.com.

We will soon have full transcripts of the CDs available in booklet form.

Chapter Recap

- Clays tournaments are great fun and an exceptional way to test your habits.

- Plan a rough schedule of tournaments at the beginning of the year, and earmark some for the best of your performances, where you will have full commitment to optimum preparation.

- Experience gained by traveling to tournaments can elevate

the scores of very good shooters who can't seem to break into the 90s consistently.

- Pre-tournament practice should be designed to build confidence, trust in your routine, and feel. Shoot easy pairs, but do so with the utmost intensity. And put the gun down two or three days before the tournament. Believe in all the hard work you've put in.

- In our experience, getting good rest is the most critical ingredient.

- Learn to read targets from the point of view of the target setter. What is the target setter trying to make you do?

- On game day, focus on what you can control: your emotions, your pre-shot and post-shot routines, your move and mount, and what you focus on during a shot. Nothing else matters.

- The scoreboard doesn't matter one damn bit until you have finished the last shot on the last station. You can't control how many targets you've already hit or missed, so focus on other things.

“The only time that you fail is when you learn nothing.”

CHAPTER FOURTEEN

AFTER *the* FAT LADY SINGS

After a tournament, you'll have a score. Oh, how we want to worship score. And there will be a challenge whether you think you scored well or not. The challenge if you don't think you scored well is staying objective in your analysis and avoiding the trap of attaching your self-worth to that number. The score is nothing more than a reflection of the quality of your move, your preparation in practice, your ability to trust and commit to the plan, and your attitude toward failure. Analyze each shot and the tournament overall by those standards. How did your move rate? Your preparation? Your ability to trust? Your attitude toward failure?

Some of the performances that we consider to be our best were not necessarily our highest scores, but those performances where we overcame adversity and found out what it takes for us to put misses behind us and finish well. The only time that you fail is when you learn nothing.

The best competitors always learn more from a perceived failure than from success. They take the time to consider the lessons they've learned, and in the final analysis, they focus on the things they did well. They are excited about what they've learned and solving the problems that came about, but they don't dwell on the failures. Sometimes they barely even remember them.

One of our shooters, Dean Olson, remarked that one memorable performance for him had to do with not remembering a target that he'd missed. Mind you, he missed fewer than 10 targets, but he was so consumed with each shot and staying in the present that by the end of it, he'd completely forgotten about one of the few shots he'd missed. Even though that meant his score was lower than he thought, it was a huge accomplishment for him.

Now, some folks may ask, what could possibly be challenging about scoring well? We've said that the voice takes many different faces, and although it loves to come in and beat you up and focus on the negative after a less-than-stellar performance, it can do just the opposite after a peak performance. If you don't believe us, take a listen to yourself and others when given a compliment after **shooting well**.

"Hey, that was great shooting out there!" says the compliment giver.

"Well, I couldn't hit the tower shot to save my life," says you.

Or

"Yeah, I think a lot of it was luck."

Or

"I don't know, fourth place isn't exactly great."

We don't want to look too confident after all, because what if we can't do that at the next one? In our effort to appear gracious and downplay our success, we often do the same thing we do after a failure: dwell on everything that went wrong.

This affects a lot of us, because most people expect so much of themselves. Sporting clays magnifies this because even when you win, or perform well at the highest level, there are almost always three or four targets that you know you have the capability to hit, but didn't.

So self-talk after a successful performance is just as important. Our advice: rather than downplaying your success or just saying "thank you" when someone congratulates you, attach that "thank you" to some of the reasons you shot well. For example: "I focused well today, I really saw the birds. I was happy with the breakpoints I picked. I felt a solid connection to the targets."

Whatever you feel contributed the most, name it. It could be that your routine was exceptional. Or possibly that you were able to create the zone before the tournament ever began. Maybe you had more trust than you've ever had, or your practice sessions leading up to the tournament were great.

Vocalizing these types of phrases is a reaffirmation that will make it easier in your next performance to do the very same thing. Think about the way it felt, the way it looked, how it happened. It's okay to say, "Yes, I shot well today." But if you don't attach that gratitude to what created the performance, it's an open door for the voice to come in and say, "Yeah, you did it today, but what will happen if you don't do as well next time?"

Have your own little list of the top ten things you really do well when you have a successful performance. Go back through your past performances and write it down. That's why we harp on keeping a log. If you'll keep a simple log, it'll help to keep the negative thinking in check. If you begin to write down these things and use them every time you have a good performance, we think you'll find that your low scores will become higher, which will also push your high scores up.

Just Rewards

There's one last thing we advocate after a big tournament season: take some time to reward yourself and your family. You're sacrificing a lot of spare time in order to train for and travel to these events. Your family is supporting you in something that makes you less available to them. If you don't stop at least a few times a year and take a week off to go fishing, spend some time with your family, or whatever you do to reward yourself, you're once again laying out a welcome mat for the voice.

Allow yourself some idle time. Let your family know you appreciate their support. Reflect on how far you've come, and think about all the things you've learned. The perspective you gain from it will make you a better shooter and a lot more fun to be around.

Chapter Recap

- A tournament score is nothing more than a reflection of the quality of your move, your preparation in practice, your ability to trust and commit to the plan, and your attitude toward failure on that particular day.

- You always learn more from a failure than a success.

- Learning to deal effectively with success and compliments is just as important to thought management as learning to deal with failure.

- When you succeed, attach your gratitude to the things that created that success.

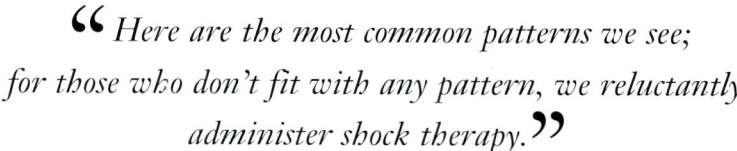

" Here are the most common patterns we see; for those who don't fit with any pattern, we reluctantly administer shock therapy."

CHAPTER FIFTEEN

COMMON CHALLENGES

When you have worked with thousands of shooters as well as other top performers, you tend to feel like a psychiatrist after a while, especially since so much of this game (as well as life itself) takes place in your head. When it comes to challenges, there are some very definite patterns that form in sporting clays. While everything is one big obstacle for beginning shooters, many intermediate shooters experience the same specific types of obstacles. And challenges become even more specific for advanced shooters, since they have fewer. Here are the most common patterns we see; for those who don't fit with any pattern, we reluctantly administer shock therapy.

Intermediate Shooters

We classify intermediate shooters as those with tournament averages between 70 and 79. The most immediate obstacle they face at the beginning of a shooting year is too much gun movement. They're moving the gun vertically first, instead of laterally. The urge to get right into practicing pairs and "tougher targets" is usually a big reason for this.

As an intermediate shooter, it's important to remember that you're still building a move database, working to etch it into your subconscious. That means it's important to do quite a bit of move training. But most shooters at this level are chomping at the bit to compete with the big boys, and they think they should start practicing pairs immediately. They'll do some move training shooting single targets, but they'll focus on the presentations that are easiest for them to hit instead of looking for weakness targets. Then they'll go right to shooting tons of pairs and long shots, instead of singles within thirty yards.

Many intermediate shooters we see are not spending enough time building that move database, and they tend to shoot tournaments too early in the year, before the fundamentals are fully greased. It's important to understand that you will never shoot better than the quality of your basic move and mount, so if your fundamental move is average, you are resigned to mediocre shooting regardless of how many pairs or forty-yard tower shots you practice.

This leads right into another common problem for intermediates, which is excessive muzzle awareness. Because their swing mechanics are still fairly conscious, it's easy for the brain to go the barrels. When this happens, the eyes come off the target. Either that, or the barrel sneaks much closer to the target and blocks the vision. Playing away from the bird is a skill they have yet to master.

Another big challenge for intermediate shooters is balancing commitment with expectation. This isn't usually a big problem for advanced shooters because they've already learned the lessons of commitment. It takes a strong commitment to become an 85 to 95 percent shooter. It takes dedication to move training and altering attitudes toward change and learning from failure. But intermediate shooters often expect to be performing as well as the advanced shooters they know, often without an equal commitment.

At the beginning of the year, intermediate shooters sometimes expect to pick up right where they left off before the season ended the year before. But without the move database of an advanced shooter and a detailed shooting log, you shouldn't expect to pick up right where you left off. As a mid-level shooter, it will take burning some powder to get to that point. Be patient with yourself. Learn to control your emotions, and look at every failure as an opportunity to learn. Use your log to help you take something good away from every performance.

Suggestions for the Intermediate

In light of everything above, here are a few specific parts of the game that we'd recommend focusing on:

- The reciprocal move. For a right-hander, this is a left-to-right presentation and just the opposite for a lefty. The reason we advocate practicing this move more is because the hands have to work in opposite directions. In our opinion, you can't practice it too much. The back hand—the timing hand—should be programmed to bring the gun smoothly to your face, while the front hand—the tempo hand—is trained to push the muzzles to the breakpoint.
- The lateral move. Every movement the muzzle makes should be laterally toward the breakpoint. This is most lacking at the beginning of the year, after many of us have been bird hunting. You'll want to go vertical instead of lateral.
- Stretching peripheral acceptance of the gun. We hit on this earlier when we talked about playing away from the bird.

Remember how we said the peripheral acceptance of an intermediate is two to four feet, where it's 12 to 30 feet for an advanced shooter? So it's important to slowly stretch your comfort level playing further ahead of the target. Get that gun way out front and see what it feels like. Practice on Zone One targets (Chapter 11, *If It Ain't Broke, Fix It!*) Get your rhythm and feel down, and begin to stretch that peripheral acceptance.

As an intermediate shooter, you have to learn to let the gun move well in front of the bird as they both head toward the breakpoint. If you let the bird get too close to the gun, the muzzle is now in your immediate periphery and you'll get jammed; it will block your vision and cause you to wonder how you missed when everything looked so right. Start slowly and stay farther in front of the bird ... farther in front of the bird ... farther out in front of the bird. This allows you to move the gun more slowly so you can feel it better. It also allows you to mount the gun slower. And when you see the bird, it's important that not only you begin to move the muzzles to the breakpoint, but that you begin the mount so that you don't have to panic at the end and get the gun up.

- Train the move, train the move, train the move. Single bird, single bird, single bird. Move the breakpoint. Single bird, single bird, single bird. Move the breakpoint. There isn't a need to practice advanced presentations until you've mastered the fundamentals. Start on the simple ones and then slowly start working toward those with more speed and distance. Remember to have soft grip pressure. Many intermediates grip the gun much too tightly.

Intermediate Shooters Mid-Year

It's certain that you've heeded the advice to spend the majority of your time in practice training the move, right? So at this point, you'll probably have four of the six basic trajectories down pat, with two that you still need to train on. The six basic trajectories are left-to-right and right-to-left crossers, left-to-right and right-to-left quartering birds, birds going up (teal), and birds coming down (falling teal). Isolate the two presentations you're weakest on, and train on them until they are firmly rooted in your subconscious.

At mid-year, it's a good time to reassess the goals you set at the beginning. Have you achieved your short-term goals? Are you on track for those in the long-term? Go back to your log and look for patterns of success and failure in your tournaments. These are simply signs that help you get to advanced levels.

It's a good idea to seek help from your coach at this point. He or she can assist you in nitpicking your move and working on your attitude and emotions. Trust the advice. If coach tells you not to worry about something, don't worry about it. If he tells you to go out and shoot 1,500 left-to-right crossers, don't stop at 1,000. There's a reason. The reason a coach tells you to go do something is because it has resulted in success many times before. Yes, we have a practice just like a lawyer or a doctor; we're practicing coaches. We're always learning just as you are, but our goal is to give you the best chance for success. An educated guess from a coach will probably be more effective than trying to do everything yourself or listening to your buddies.

Concentrate on your self-talk. It's time to bring it to a higher level. It has to always be solution-oriented, in the fewest words possible, and a statement of what you are going to do to break the next target. Be consumed with the process, not the outcome. Be consumed with how your move feels. Be consumed with how good the timing is. Be consumed with how easy it is for you to maintain focus on the front of that target. Be consumed with how softly and slowly your eyes go from soft focus on the target to hard focus on the front edge when it's about two thirds of the way to the breakpoint. Be excited to learn from the failures if you want them to go away.

An Intermediate Log

The log for an intermediate shooter will probably have quite a bit to do with mechanical issues because the majority of their work has to do with building that mechanical database. It's still a necessity to think about what the gun is doing. That increases awareness of the gun during training and practice. It's okay. Accept it. Resistance is ineffective. Write down your observations of the mechanical game. Go through the conscious competence phase until you begin to feel a connection to the target as you move with it.

In your log, review the hurdles you had to overcome the year before. Don't fear problems, because you'll see them again in different forms. That's one thing we've learned in working with so many different students: you will have one or two things that come back to haunt you at every plateau. But that's okay, because once you know what it is, you know where to go.

So write down your strengths and weaknesses from the year before. Try to be as objective as possible in facing the reality of where you are now. Work within the goals and commitments that you've made. Use the log to train on your weaknesses. Instead of shooting feel-good targets, shoot the ones that cause you the most problems. Train to eliminate weaknesses.

When you begin to get your feel back after the beginning of the year, start to work on your pre-shot routine. Do that once you're back in the flow of things. At the start, be consumed with the fundamentals. But you don't want to start doing your practice routine and shooting pairs, pairs, pairs, until you've gotten back into the gun on the six basic trajectories. It takes a lot of hard work and determination to build a database, one shot at a time.

Once you do begin performance practice, remember that it's ultimately about controlling the thought process. It's hard enough to do this when you've done something a thousand times, but it's truly a challenge when you've only done it a few times. So be forgiving and work on six pairs in a row, change the presentation, six pairs in a row, change the presentation, etc.

Write down the quality of your practice sessions in your log. Be determined in those sessions. Practice is not play. Playing is fine if that's what you're going to do. Go play. But if you go to train and practice, do it with the fire in your eye that you'd have on tournament day. You can't be trying to break the targets on game day. On game day you must be breaking them at the breakpoints and trusting your ability via your practice routine and your pre-shot routine, because if you're trying to break the targets, you're thinking about swing mechanics and lead.

Have we mentioned the importance of stretching your peripheral acceptance? Well, good. The more we coach, the more we realize that 99 percent of errors don't come from mechanical problems, but from blocking the vision in one or both eyes. Ninety-nine percent of the time a target is missed, the root cause is lack of focus. Not necessarily lack of sharp focus on the target, although that is common, but from letting the muzzle block out your peripheral circle. Be aware that the gun is going to get in the way during the intermediate phase. It's okay. It'll get in the way less and less as you train more, provided you get the gun farther and farther out and let the target come to you. Instead of chasing the target with the muzzle, try catching it with the muzzle like an outfielder would catch a fly ball.

Advanced Shooters

We generally classify advanced shooters as those with tournament averages between 85 and 95. Now, we know all the accountants out there will say we've got a six-bird gap between our intermediate average of 72–79 and advanced scores between 85 and 95. In our experience, once a shooter passes 79, it's a rapid transition to 85. You rarely find shooters with a consistent average between 80 and 84, because once you break the hold of conscious engineering and mechanical thought, you begin to trust and begin to feel. This means the fundamentals are ingrained in your subconscious. We've found that this takes you through 80 to 84 extremely fast.

If you're an advanced shooter who averaged between 85 and 95 the year before, a loss of timing typically occurs at the beginning of the new shooting year. This has occurred because they've been out hunting and shooting wild birds. When you're shooting wild birds, you rarely have a breakpoint; it occurs whenever the gun touches your face. So there is a simple loss of timing and feel. The remedy for this is to concentrate on that lateral move rather than vertical. Another thing that tends to slip is keeping your eyes still before calling for the bird, or moving prior to focusing on the bird.

The two birds that advanced shooters typically have the most difficulty with are the rising quartering bird (on the right side for righties and the left for lefties) and the teal, because you can't see the bird when you pull the trigger if the gun is in the right spot.

Our advice is to single out a crossing trajectory that is fairly simple, work on a breakpoint, and look to regain as much feel as possible. You have the fundamental database down, so it's only a matter of getting back into feel mode and trust mode. Once you master feel on that target, move through all six trajectories.

Shoot medium length and close targets before you start stretching it out. Move the breakpoints. Once you can break them 10 times in a row in the same spot with feel, move on to performance practice. Your move and mount must be in sync with the speed of the bird and the timing in the breakpoint so that you know the bird is dead before it gets to the breakpoint. This is where confidence and consistency come from. Confidence and consistency cannot be practiced. They are the residue of practice. Consistency comes from confidence. Confidence is the absence of doubt—the absence of the voice. When your move is in sync with the target and you know are you going to break it in the breakpoint *before* it gets there, you **become confident**. At this point, there is *no voice* in your head talking about swing mechanics or lead. There are only targets and breakpoints connected by your move. Welcome to the zone.

One thing that differs big time from our advice for intermediate shooters is that advanced shooters should shoot a competition as soon as possible. If you're an advanced shooter, shooting a tournament right away will certainly show you what dragons you're going to have to slay this year. When you're a shooter in the 80s and 90s, there are typically not many dragons in practice, but when you go to competition, you see what face they're going to wear.

An Advanced Log
The log for an advanced shooter should create a realistic assessment of the previous year, including the amount of commitment it took to create whatever level of performances you had. It should also allow for more specific goals at the start of a new year. You can look at what it took last year and base your new goals and commitments on that information. It's a good idea to look at several of the previous year's entries in your log.

Look for common problems. Look for patterns that you went through or evidence of similar mistakes each year. The advanced shooter typically will create a better plan to start their year because they've learned from any mistakes the year before and kept a detailed log. Most advanced shooters also have no fear of getting it back. But a few in this category are afraid to put the gun down and take a break during the off-season. In our experience, you'll have a lull mid-summer if you do this, and sometimes it turns into a slump. Put the gun down and do something else. Take a break. You will be stronger for it.

There's no reason to have fear of getting it back if you're an advanced shooter. You got it back last year and you can get it back this year. Fear is not a good emotion to drive you when you're trying to learn or perform.

Advanced at Mid-Year

As an advanced shooter at mid-year, you'll begin to refine your focus on the target, and you'll begin to refine your mental focus. As you get back into the gun and shoot more tournaments, you'll be able to push the bar higher for both those aspects. You've now trained your eyes back into the condition they were in at the end of last year. Your routine has become more comfortable, more subconscious, and you've gotten back into your database of feel.

Now is the time to work on controlling your emotions and your expectations. This is where the self-talk phrases come in so well. Use them, use them, use them. In our opinion, advanced shooters should meet with their coach once a month to talk about thoughts and emotions in the overall game. Find out what it takes for you to get yourself into the zone before you ever step into a stand.

Just like intermediate shooters, a mid-year assessment is in order. Have you achieved any short-term goals? Is change needed due to unforeseen circumstances? Are you ahead of your goal? Let's say your goal was to have three top-five finishes by mid-year. If you've already had four, then you should know what to do: make another goal. If you don't, you probably won't be in the top five any more.

Advanced shooters should also focus intently on improving the quality of their practice sessions. Train on the move with intensity, and practice performance with even more intensity. It's true that the ratio of performance practice will be much greater than the move training for you, but remember to always train on one of the six basic moves every time you go out to practice. That doesn't mean you have to shoot ten boxes of shells, maybe you'll just shoot one, but if you neglect training on the fundamentals, they will begin to slip. Grade the move and rate the feel. When you move to performance practice, shoot six pairs in a row. They don't have to be hard, but it should be like you to run six pairs in a row. Usually, on game day, it's no more than three or four, but you'll be used to hitting six pairs.

One thing that can befall advanced shooters more than others is the overpracticing syndrome. Usually this has to do with the sheer number of targets they're shooting at one practice session. They'll go out and blast through a flat of ammo for one session. This is fine in certain situations, but making a habit of it will probably not help your game. We recommend shooting fewer shots in practice, but practicing more frequently and with the highest quality. Pay attention to the quality of the session. When your body gives you signs that the quality is slipping, hang it up. At your level, so much can be accomplished at home. Visualization with feel and practicing your gun mount fifty times a night will do much more for your game than going to the range and blasting yourself to exhaustion.

> **Willy Shoots His Weaknesses**
>
> *We talked to Willy Cherry about his mix of move training and performance practice, his log, and shooting his weaknesses. He told us that he realized most of his practice the year before, probably 90 percent, was spent on move training.*
>
> *"I think that was one of the reasons I spent so much time being mechanical," he said. "Since then, it's like I can't wait to write in my log. It has changed so many things in how I go out to the practice field."*
>
> *Specifically, Willy mentioned setting up a practice course that did nothing but exploit the weaknesses he'd been noticing. "It was a really great day," he said. "I didn't shoot a great score, but compared to what I was doing last year, it was a month's worth of practice in one day. It was just really neat."*
>
> *Keeping a log and focusing on your weaknesses is a great way to break out of a flatline in your practice. Chances are, if you've hit a plateau in your practice, you've hit a plateau in your performance as well.*

The last bit of advice we have for advanced shooters is to practice the mental game as much, if not more, than the physical game. Do it everywhere. Work on self-talk. Make visualization an everyday thing. Be aware of your emotional reactions in different situations. Set a non-judgmental mindset at the beginning of every day, and see how well you preserve it. If you can stay happy or neutral at work and with your family, you're giving yourself a much better chance to stay that way when you shoot.

Remember, it is what it is. It becomes what you make it.

Chapter Recap

- Most shooters at similar levels tend to face common challenges. For intermediate shooters (70-79) one of those is too much gun movement at the beginning of the year.

- Intermediate shooters also don't spend enough time building a move database, shooting pairs too much in their practice ratio.

- Excessive muzzle awareness is another very common problem for intermediates. Playing away from the bird is the cure.

- Balancing commitment with expectation is another point of difficulty. Many intermediate shooters expect to shoot as well as their advanced counterparts without an increase in commitment.

- Our suggestions for intermediate shooters include: focusing on the reciprocal move (left-to-right for a right-hander); moving laterally to the breakpoint on each shot; stretching peripheral awareness; and continuing to train the fundamentals.

- Advanced shooters (85-95) typically experience a loss of timing at the beginning of the shooting year. The cure is to single out a simple trajectory and work on breakpoint until the feel begins to return. Then begin stretching the distance.

- We suggest that advanced shooters go out and compete as soon as possible at the start of a year, whereas we advise intermediates to wait a while.

- At mid-year, advanced shooters should really begin working on controlling emotions and expectations, putting self-talk phrases to good use. Practice the mental game just as much as the mechanical game.

> *There is nothing wrong with mechanical instruction, but the trick for coaches is to get the student to listen to these mechanical instructions without judgment, doubt, or fear.*

CHAPTER SIXTEEN

COACHING FEEL

We are all coaches. If you have kids, you're a coach. If you have pets, you're a coach. If you've ever whistled and heard someone else start whistling, too, you're a coach. We all model each other all the time, whether we know it or not. And we're constantly coaching not only others, but ourselves. This is why it's important to understand how to coach feel.

Many advanced shooters reading this are probably certified instructors or are constantly giving advice to others. Even if you aren't now, it's a likely possibility you might be coaching in the future. So we'd like to share what we've learned about the process of coaching, and we hope it will help you become better coaches to yourselves and others.

In our opinion, the best coaches are simply mirrors and spotlights. As mirrors they help the student see what is there, rather than what the student thinks is there. As spotlights, they help the students focus on whatever aspect of that reality would be the most beneficial in the current moment. This is why you'll hear us ask our students a lot of questions. How still did your eyes feel? How tight were your hands? Did you feel connected to the target? Did you feel like the bird was coming to you, or were you chasing the bird? These phrases are not commands, but by making the student aware of a specific aspect of their game, they will serve as corrections. In almost every case, the subconscious will make corrections without the coach ever saying "do" or "don't."

> **"Learning via discovery imprints more quickly than learning via directives."**
> —*Gil and Vicki Ash*

Sure, you could say, "Keep your eyes still," or "Don't move your eyes," but these are instructions that the ego tends to resist. And remember what we said about the subconscious and the word "don't?" Wasn't it easy to not picture those little green men on your leg?

Focus on Feel Rather Than Results

If you are obsessed with whether the student broke the target, the student will be, too. In practice, it doesn't matter at all whether the student broke the target. Yes, almost every student you'll coach will think that it matters, but it doesn't. No one is keeping score. Do what you can to keep the student focused on what it feels like.

Instruction that is non-judgmental is always the most effective. You can't make your student non-judgmental, but you can model what it's like to be non-judgmental. When there is no fear or doubt embedded in the learning process, it'll be easy. Let your student know that you have complete confidence in their ability to self-correct. That's why you have an attitude of exploration. Is overtightness bad? No, but if it's there, let's see if we can find out more about it. Let's be aware of it.

That's why the first exercise we recommend for building feel is to start out shooting a simple target with only one goal: make absolutely no corrections. Just observe what is there. It doesn't matter whether the target breaks or not, that's not the goal. The goal is to shoot without making one single correction. It's usually more challenging than it sounds.

Speak a Visual Language

There is nothing wrong with mechanical instruction, but the trick for coaches is to get the student to listen to these mechanical instructions without judgment, doubt, or fear. The student should understand that relying too heavily on instructions will eventually hamper their ability to feel. Mechanical knowledge is the most effective when it gives a hint of a desired destination. For example: "See if any imbalance occurs during the shot, and if so, try to pinpoint the spot where it occurs." Obviously, the desired destination is balance, and this might be a great way to get the student to change stance or posture without giving them an order. A lot of technique can be learned merely by paying attention to your body as it moves with the gun.

Remember that you're using the student's conscious mind to deliver information to the subconscious, because it's the subconscious that is responsible for the move, mount and taking the shot. That's why using visual instructions is key. Stevie Ray Brown has a perfect example of this. He told us about putting on a clinic for instructors in Dallas.

There were several instructors watching one student shoot, and they all knew that the student was moving much too fast to break the target. The instructor working directly with the student continually told him to slow down, and each time the student agreed that he would slow down, but then he'd call pull and move like a man on fire. Stevie wanted to make a point so he let it continue until both the instructor and the student were in a pretty deep hole. Then he stepped in and said, "Class, I want you to remember what is about to happen. Remember this." He looked at the student and said, "Where you from, Doc?"

"Weatherford, Texas," the guy replied.

Stevie asked him, "Out in Weatherford, do they have any sorghum molasses?"

The student said, "Yes."

Stevie said, "And in the winter it gets pretty cold out there, right?" Another yes. "How about February?" Stevie asked.

"It's a cold month," the student replied.

Stevie said, "Okay, now I want you to move with this target like molasses coming out of that jar in February."

The fellow slowed down and broke the target. Stevie was able to give his subconscious an image, whereas the instructor-in-training was giving him a word. But the subconscious didn't understand s-l-o-w. A few of the many visual instructions we give shooters include: reach out and touch the target with the gun (for quartering), kiss the bird with that gun (for soft moves), or dance with the target (to match the target's rhythm and relax.)

Encourage Independent Experimentation

Another trap that coaches can fall into is creating students who are dependent on them. This usually isn't intentional, but it does happen often because of our traditional understanding of how to coach. Coaches give commands and students follow them in this system, but it's our experience that the best tool we can give our students is simply a belief in their own natural ability, in the ability of the subconscious to take care of their movements. You can make as many commands as you want, but until a student trusts himself and chooses to listen, your breath is wasted. Good instruction should be empowering. One of the best ways to empower a student is to encourage experimentation. This is how we came to understand what we understand as coaches—through experimentation. If students are going to be good self-coaches, learning to experiment is essential.

For example, a good exercise to get a feel for muzzle placement during a shot is to intentionally shoot too far ahead of the target. This means your goal is to miss the target in front. How far in front do you have to be to actually miss in front? This is a wonderful experiment for feel. What does it feel like when you're that far out? The same experiment can be played out by shooting behind, above, and below the target. This also helps a student detach score from self-worth because it creates a new game where score is unimportant.

Something that has worked well for some athletes is actually turning the shot over to the subconscious by saying show me how to break this bird. That is a perfect experiment for absolute trust in the subconscious.

Another good experiment for feel is to break a target by moving in the opposite way you normally would. For example, if it's a left-to-right crosser, you move to the breakpoint from right-to-left instead of heading in the same direction as the bird. This type of experiment allows the student to miss without judgment. It gets them out of the box of worrying so much about whether the target breaks or not and makes feel the priority. Anything you can come up with that will produce this effect is a good experiment.

Here is a brilliant experiment we've adapted from Tim Gallwey's *Inner Game of Golf*. The next time you compete against friends or in a tournament that is just for fun, give yourself a certain score that you're not allowed to shoot above. Let's say you average 75. Set a score that's somewhere around there, maybe a 73, and do not allow yourself to shoot better than that. If you get to the last station and you've already broken 73, you have to drop all the remaining targets. Don't tell anyone what you're doing, and don't let on that you aren't taking your score seriously. Do everything you normally would do to break targets, until you approach your pre-set score. At that point you must do whatever is necessary to make sure you don't overtake that score. This is difficult to do, especially if you're shooting better than you ever have before. But watch how everyone else is impacted by your score, and how seriously they take it. Become an objective observer to the drama that is playing out in your own game. It's a great experiment for understanding that pressure is entirely self-induced. The goal is to create this tournament mindset: **Shoot the targets as if your life depended on it, and then be able to leave the performance behind in an instant.**

For students who take the game too seriously, have them shoot 25 or 50 targets purely for maximum enjoyment, regardless of score. If that means shooting targets from the hip, let them shoot from the hip. If that means shooting them with eyes closed, let them close their eyes. Maybe they want to holler like a Mexican vaquero after every shot. Whatever they want to do for fun, let them do it. The goal in this experiment is pure play, to make every shot as much fun as it can possibly be. It helps to bring a student back to the idea that this is *a game*.

One last word on this: remember that the genius is in the student, not the coach. True coaching has nothing to do with the coach. You're just lending a hand in their discovery and should be equally enthralled with the process, because it's going to affect you as well. You are just as much a student as they are. Every student has the potential to give you insight that could change your life and your capacity to coach. The most important question a student or a coach can ever ask is: What did I learn?

Chapter Recap

- The most effective coaching is awareness instruction, where the coach serves as a mirror to show the student what is actually occurring and spotlights the aspects that would be the most beneficial to change.

- When coaching, focus on feel. Make that of primary importance, and the student will, too. One good exercise for building feel is to shoot a target where the only goal is to make no corrections, but to simply observe what is there.

- Avoid judgments of good or bad. Maintain an attitude of exploration.

- A coach uses the student's conscious mind to deliver information to the subconscious. This is done most effectively with detailed pictures.

- Encourage experimentation. This is how good shooters become great shooters and good coaches become great coaches.

- Remember that the genius lies with the student, not with the coach.

> *Overall, the most important aspect of a review is to focus specifically on patterns of peak performances, regardless of what the score was or where you placed.*

CHAPTER SEVENTEEN

REVIEWING YOUR YEAR

The end of a shooting year is where the log pays off big time. It's one of the most important times to review your log and also one of the most important times to write in it. This is just as much a part of success in shooting as your practice and tournament experience. If you neglect it, there is a high probability that it will bite you in the ass.

As you go back through your log and review your year, look for recurring problems and recurring success. When you find a pattern like that, ask "why?" What was it that contributed to the problems or the success? The end of the year isn't the only time where it's good to do this, but it's especially important to do it at the end of the year.

When we go through our students' logs, we're always looking for a relationship between the quality and frequency of practice and the quality of tournament performances. Take a look at how you scheduled tournaments and how you scheduled practices. Think about the other non-shooting-related priorities that were going on: weddings, home remodeling, business concerns, etc. How well did your schedule for the year allow you to prepare for tournaments, especially those that were intended for peak performances?

It's also a good idea to look at the total number of tournaments that you shot. What was the relationship and sequence of big tournaments and small tournaments? Did you shoot a small tournament the week before Nationals? How did you feel about that? Did you shoot two big tournaments back to back? Were your performances superior at bigger tournaments or smaller tournaments? It's crucial that you look for individual patterns at the end of the year, because that's how you set your new goals.

In our opinion, it's also important to know the total number of registered targets that you shot. Separate the targets that were shot in different events—sporting clays targets from the five stand targets from FITASC targets from small gauge targets. Identify patterns here as well. If you went to a shoot and did well in small gauges and five stand but did the backstroke through the sewer lagoon in the main event and FITASC, maybe your body was trying to tell you something. You might be shooting too many events.

We'd also recommend that you be somewhat aware of the total number of practice targets you shot and the frequency of your sessions. Did the frequency or duration change when you moved to pre-tournament practice? How about the frequency of your lessons from a coach? If you took a lesson, how did it affect your practice and performance down the road? Did it take long to institute something new? That should give you some clue as to whether you should take a lesson two weeks before a tournament. Sometimes students will come to us just before a tournament and say, "Don't change me, just tweak me." That's fine, and we'll put a band-aid on any potential issues. But typically, if you come to us, we're going to look for any weaknesses so you can then make it a strength.

Overall, the most important aspect of a review is to focus specifically on patterns of peak performances, regardless of what the score was or where you placed. If you felt that it was a peak performance, analyze it. The reason we stress these patterns? Because they hold the answer to how you best prepare your mind and body for optimum performance. It will be different for each one of you, and that's why an individual log is so effective.

Goal Check

Once you've reviewed your year, we recommend taking a look back at the goals you set as well. Did you achieve short-term or long-term goals? What led to the achievement or got in the way? Was it a change in practice? Was it something you learned in a lesson? Was it a change in routine? Improved visualization? Non-shooting-related priorities? Do your best to understand the factors that contributed to achieving a goal or not achieving a goal.

If a goal wasn't achieved, it's okay. That's simply a signal that an adjustment is needed. You should have a good idea what that adjustment is, based on what you've learned from your performances over the past year.

It's equally important to take action if you achieved your goals. Any goal that was achieved should be replaced with a new one before you head into the off-season. If you don't set a new goal or reaffirm old ones, it will be very difficult to have any direction once you begin the new season. Yes, any goal you make now can change; in fact, it probably will change, but we feel that it's important to get it down at the end of the year. Remember that specific goals are usually the most effective, and you'll make it easier on yourself if you base them off your current improvement curve. If you're averaging in the high 80s, winning a big shoot isn't a bad short-term goal to set. But if you're shooting in the high 70s, winning a big shoot may be an over-inflated expectation based on how quickly you've been progressing, especially if your commitment is going to remain the same. Any new goals or adjustments to old goals should be accompanied with a change in commitment.

Go ahead and start making your tournament schedule for the following year. Sure, it's going to change too, but go ahead and make it. Put a tentative schedule in writing, along with a rough training and practice schedule. In order to improve, there will have to be some change in your commitment to practice time, to quality practice time, and to take lessons.

The Most Important Question

Let's see if you're paying attention. Anyone remember what we wrote just 1,124 short words ago about the most important question a student or coach can ever ask? Well, now is the time to ask it: "What did I learn?" After you have reviewed your log, or during the review if you prefer, we suggest making a list of everything that you've learned over the year. For example, if you had a problem trajectory, how did you turn it into a strength? How did you overcome the first-station jitters? Whatever hurdles you jumped, write them down, and write down how you got over them. Was it something small like changing glasses, guns, or ammo? Was it a matter of getting better sleep, changing your diet, or getting more exercise?

This is a great time to get in the habit of thinking hard and often about your best performances. The more time and energy you spend analyzing and envisioning them, the better the chances that you will have more.

Chapter Recap

- A well-maintained shooting log pays off big at the end of the shooting year. In reviewing your log, look for patterns and ask why they occurred.

- Keep an eye out for a relationship between the quality and frequency of your practice and the quality of your tournament performances.

- Get an idea of how many tournaments you shot, the total number of registered targets, and a good estimate of how many practice targets over the year.

- Have a look back at your goals for the year. Try to understand the factors that allowed goals to be accomplished or blocked you from accomplishing them.

- Any goal that was accomplished should be replaced with a new goal.

- Write down the things that you learned over the year.

"Believe enough in yourself and your game that you can let go of every instruction and simply react to the target."

Chapter Eighteen

Parting Thoughts

Here we are at 180 pages, time for a conclusion ... and we were just warming up. Of course there's more to come, which shouldn't come as a shock to those who know us. If Gil has his way, this series might run longer than the Bible. But we'll let you chew on this one for now, and end with a few parting thoughts.

The True Keys to Consistency

You give yourself the best chance for consistent improvement in this game when you constantly refine your mechanics to higher and higher subconscious levels and constantly increase your ability to completely forget about mechanics at will. Anything you can do to enhance feel will help you on both those fronts. The things that create the best environment for feel include focus (your relaxed concentration in the stand), tempo (always moving in concert with the target), trust (your belief in the strength of your mechanics and practice) and rhythm (your pre-shot, post-shot, and correction routines). Believe enough in yourself and your game that you can let go of every instruction and simply react to the target. You are only limited by your ability to trust your subconscious.

This Is Just a Game, and Much More

Like any good game, the one we play is both silly and divine. Everything we do in life is an opportunity to become fully present, to live fully in the moment, and shotgunning is no different. The beauty is, the only time you perform to your full potential is when you are fully present. So step into that station like you're the first shotgunner to ever shoot a clay. Allow yourself to be there, to really feel it, to truly be amazed by what it is you're doing. Because it is amazing. Be thankful that there is a game to play and that you have the time and means to actively pursue excellence as you define it. Understand that every shot is a new creation, because every stand is a new creation. When your goal is to repeat a shot or performance from the past, that's fear talking. It means you're afraid you can't create an equally good shot or performance. But you can do that—it just takes a full commitment to each shot, and that is what feel is really all about. That is how you play "out of your mind." If you try to turn yourself into a Xerox machine instead and replicate the same move over and over, your mind will rebel by abandoning focus. Trying to repeat the exact same swing is not only conscious but boring. When was the last time you did anything exceptional when you were bored?

Remember that all of these things hold true for your business and your family and any other hobbies as well. You are the artist of your own life. You're creating it as you go. Most people rob themselves of power by letting their past dictate their future, but extraordinary people do not let their circumstances bind them. They have the ability to turn every day of their lives into a new creation. Identify the parts of yourself that do not change, the aspects that truly reflect who you are, and allow your shooting to be a reflection of that. Allow everything you do to be a reflection of that. Yes, we're getting a little Oprah on you here, but we truly believe in this stuff.

We truly believe that this system of mental performance and thought management can be applied to just about any game, especially those with a lot of variables. And the only game we can think of with more variables than sporting clays is the game of life.

Enough reading. Go out and play.